1991

INSTRUCTIONAL MANAGEMENT

INSTRUCTIONAL MANAGEMENT

For Detecting and Correcting Special Problems

Joyce S. Choate/Series Consulting Editor
Northeast Louisiana University

WILLIAM H. EVANS
University of West Florida

SUSAN S. EVANS
University of West Florida

ROBERT A. GABLE
Old Dominion University

REX E. SCHMID
Alachua County Schools

ALLYN AND BACON
Boston / London / Toronto / Sydney / Tokyo / Singapore

THE ALLYN AND BACON
DETECTING AND CORRECTING SERIES
Joyce S. Choate, *Series Consulting Editor*

Copyright © 1991 by Allyn and Bacon
A Division of Simon & Schuster, Inc.
160 Gould Street
Needham Heights, Massachusetts 02194-2310

Editorial Production Service: Karen G. Mason
Copyeditor: Susan Freese
Cover Administrator: Linda K. Dickinson
Cover Designer: Susan Slovinsky

Library of Congress Cataloging-in-Publication Data

Instructional management for detecting and correcting special problems
        / William H. Evans . . . [et al.].
            p.   cm. -- (The Allyn and Bacon detecting and correcting series)
        Includes bibliographical references.
        ISBN 0-205-12387-2
        1. Instructional systems.   2. Classroom management.   3. Behavior
modification.   4. Individualized instruction.   I. Evans, William
II. Series.
LB1028.35.I58   1990
371.1'024--dc20   90--32719

Printed in the United States of America

10 9 8 7 6 5 4 3 2 1   94 93 92 91 90

Contents

FOREWORD
ABOUT THE DETECTING AND CORRECTING SERIES

Instructional Management for Detecting and Correcting Special Problems is one of several books in an affordable series that focuses on the classroom needs of special students, both exceptional and nonexceptional, who often require adjusted methods and curricula. The purpose of this book, as well as the others in the series, is to supplement more comprehensive and theoretical treatments of major instructional issues—in this case, managing the instructional process—with practical classroom practices.

The underlying theme of each book in the *Detecting and Correcting* series is targeted instruction to maximize students' achievement. Designed for informed teachers and teachers-in-training who are responsible for instructing special students in a variety of settings, these books emphasize the application of theory to everyday classroom concerns. While this approach may not be unique, the format in which both theme and purpose are presented is such that it enables the reader to quickly translate theory into practical classroom strategies for reaching hard-to-teach students.

A consistent two-part format is followed throughout the books. Detection is addressed first, beginning with a citation of a few significant behavior characteristics and continuing with a discussion of related factors. Readers familiar with the series will, however, notice in this book a slight departure from the content and format. While the other books target specific skills, the emphasis here is on facilitating the teaching and learning of those skills through efficient and effective management of the detecting and correcting process. Thus, this book binds and enables the implementation of the strategies recommended in the other books of the series.

The simple, consistent format makes the *Detecting and Correcting* books accessible and easy to read. Other useful features include: a) the Contents organization, designed for quick location of appropriate topics and problem skills and behaviors; b) a concise explanation of skills, special needs, and guiding principles for implementing instruction; c) a "Reflections" section ending each part, providing discussion and application activities; and d) an index of general topics and cross-references to related subjects.

Effective instructional management is essential to implementing educational programs that accommodate the needs of special students. The procedures suggested for managing classroom instruction facilitate students' progress in the areas discussed in the related books—basic mathematics, classroom behavior, language arts, reading, science and health, social studies, and speech and language. Together, these books comprise an expanding series that simplifies teachers' tasks by offering sound and practical classroom procedures for detecting and correcting special needs and problems.

Joyce S. Choate
Series Consulting Editor

PREFACE

Even under the best of conditions, teaching is a demanding task. Reading, writing, language arts, social studies, and science must be taught to students who have distinctly unique learning characteristics, values, and interests. Music, art, and physical education as well as lunch and sometimes breakfast must be scheduled. Arrangements must be made for the coming and going of students who require counseling or special instruction. Assignments must be made, papers graded, conferences held, reports filed—all while maintaining a cheerful demeanor and a level of control. Given this set of conditions, no wonder even good teachers at times become fatigued and frustrated.

Teaching is, however, an extremely rewarding profession. It is exhilarating to witness a child's discovery or mastery of a concept or to observe the social and academic growth of a student who has struggled for a long time. Changes such as these rarely occur in environments that are haphazardly organized. Rather, they are the result of painstaking planning and organization. Moreover, such results attest to the importance of tailoring the instructional program to fit the individual needs of the child and not the other way around.

This text provides a framework for establishing educational settings that are efficient, effective, and rewarding. It is designed to provide an ecological approach to detecting and correcting instructional problems. As such, it addresses the ways that home, community, and school affect performance in the classroom. Most importantly, perhaps, it illustrates that instructional planning is a multifaceted process that must constantly change to meet the needs of students, parents, and teachers.

ASSUMPTIONS

The concepts and principles in this book have been drawn from a vast body of professional literature. The thrust is upon providing practical and effective techniques that can be used to detect and correct instructional problems. The basic assumptions underlying this text are:

- Each student has unique needs that must be met in the instructional program.
- Instructional settings are affected by teacher and student behavior, as well as elements from a variety of environments.
- Not every instructional problem warrants an intrusive intervention.
- Variables in the home, community, and school have a direct impact upon the classroom and must be addressed in developing and implementing an instructional management program.
- Many instructional problems can be prevented by careful planning.
- Learning is best accomplished in settings that are orderly and that use instructional procedures and materials appropriate to the student's interest and stage of learning.
- Teaching can be an intensely rewarding experience.

This book is intended to be a source of practical suggestions that can be used by all teachers. Special teachers, as well as regular education teachers, face a variety of instructional problems. Therefore, the goal is to provide a book that can be used to assist students, regardless of their labels or special needs.

ORGANIZATION

This book is divided into three parts. Each part begins with an overview that details the concepts and content to be presented. Each part ends with a section entitled "Reflections" in which activities and additional resources are provided. Throughout the text, practical examples entitled "An Instructional Problem" are provided. These vignettes serve as advance organizers and provide real-life illustrations of the content that follows.

Part I provides a conceptual framework for ecological instructional planning. Presented in this section are procedures that may be used to identify, or target, instructional problems. Practical assessment strategies used in examining these targets are also illustrated.

Part II addresses the effects that home, community, and school have upon classroom performance. A variety of methods is presented for increasing cooperative relations among parents, members of the community, school administrators, and teachers.

Part III provides a comprehensive analysis of methods that can be used in the classroom by the teacher to correct instructional problems. Preventive planning, discipline, classroom organization, time management and scheduling, instructional grouping, materials, and individualized instructional plans are all addressed in this section. Part III closes with a chapter devoted to the joy and satisfaction that can be found in teaching and ways of preventing teacher burnout.

This book is designed to provide a wide variety of practical suggestions that can be used to detect and correct instructional problems. It is not intended to answer every instructional difficulty encountered in a classroom simply because each problem and setting demands a unique solution. Rather, the text is designed to paint a picture of effective instructional environments in which the parts are harmoniously arranged to support the whole. In such an environment, education becomes a richly rewarding experience for all.

HOW TO USE THIS BOOK

This book provides a comprehensive analysis of instructional environments. The chapters on detection will assist the reader in determining when an intervention is necessary, as well as appropriate targets for interventions. Once a behavior or environmental variable has been identified and assessed, interventions in home, community, school, and classroom settings can be developed by using information from this book and the additional sources identified in the "Reflections" sections.

All interventions should be comprehensive and cautiously developed. Moreover, careful consideration should be given to the potential side effects of any intervention so as to ensure that the cure is not worse than the problem.

ACKNOWLEDGMENTS

We, the authors wish to express our deepest gratitude to Joyce Choate, for her continuous assistance and subtle reminders, and to Ray Short, for his unending patience. The suggestions offered by Tom Stritch, University of West Florida; Susan Holleran, Fort Wayne, Indiana, Public Schools; and Craig Smith, Georgia College, proved to be invaluable. Certainly, a special thanks goes to our families who have endured this project and continually supported us.

INSTRUCTIONAL MANAGEMENT

PART I

DETECTING INSTRUCTIONAL MANAGEMENT PROBLEMS

A thorough knowledge of the subject area is a necessary and critical component of good teaching, for without this knowledge, it is difficult to impart accurate and timely information to students. It is entirely possible, however, to have a complete grasp of a subject area and thoroughly fail to teach and communicate the content to students. This suggests that it is as important to know *how* to teach as it is *what* to teach.

In order to know how to teach, it is important to first know how to assess the conditions under which learning occurs. Historically, this assessment centered upon the strengths, weaknesses, and attributes of the student. Failure was often seen as a result of the student lacking some quality, such as motivation.

More recently, however, educators have realized the necessity of an ecological approach to assessment. Of prime importance is an analysis of not only the student but also the various environments surrounding the student, as well as the behaviors of others. Ecologically oriented assessment, therefore, concentrates on a variety of factors, such as the influence that home and community have upon the instructional setting; expectations of teachers, parents, and students; values; peer interactions; and types of instructional materials and groups to name but a few. With this has also come the realization that all of these factors are interrelated; thus, when one factor changes, others change as well.

The challenge then is to assess the student's entire environment, understanding that what is being assessed will be constantly changing. This necessitates that assessment be comprehensive and ongoing.

Part I of this book presents an array of ecologically oriented assessment procedures that may be used in detecting problems in learning environments. Elements of home, community, school, and classroom are carefully examined so that assessment procedures can be appropriately and accurately focused or targeted.

Chapter 1 presents a conceptual framework for the use of comprehensive and ecologically oriented assessment procedures in educational settings. The environments and patterns of behavior that affect instructional settings are carefully examined. Of prime importance is an analysis of the interrelationship of these diverse elements and their effect upon instructional settings.

Chapter 2 examines conditions and behaviors that can be targeted or serve as a focal point for further assessment. Central issues in this chapter are the selection of appropriate targets, the realization that not all problems are caused by students, and the caution that an intervention should not be implemented with every difficulty.

Chapter 3 presents an array of assessment procedures that can be used to examine behavior and environmental conditions. The necessity of continuous assessment is addressed, as is the use of data in selecting appropriate and relevant goals for students.

Part I lays a foundation for the ecological detection of instructional problems. Once detected, these problems can be corrected by the use of comprehensive interventions that address the entire educational environment. This increases the probability that teachers and students alike will find education rewarding and satisfying.

CHAPTER 1

ECOLOGICAL INSTRUCTIONAL MANAGEMENT

To say that a multitude of factors may affect student performance in the classroom is only to note the obvious. Yet what is obvious is not always successfully managed. When the learning environment is not managed appropriately, student learning is hindered, teachers become dissatisfied and frustrated, and chaos reigns. What results is an environment in which crisis management becomes an accepted daily routine, and learning becomes a matter of chance.

Simply put, *instructional management* is the process of blending behaviors and environmental variables to produce educational conditions that are rewarding and result in a maximum amount of learning accomplished in an efficient manner. While this is the goal, the reality is that even with the best teachers, there will be instances and days in which it appears that very little is accomplished or times in which it seems that any amount of effort on the part of the student or teacher is simply inadequate. In classrooms in which the instructional program is effectively managed, however, these days are the exception and not the rule. Moreover, these classrooms foster a climate of learning that extends far beyond the classroom and affects students for years after.

One of the most formidable challenges in instructional management is deciding upon a starting point for an intervention. All too often it seems that students and teachers alike are surrounded by a teeming number of insurmountable problems. A host of difficulties—such as home and peer problems, learning and behavior disorders, inadequate facilities and materials, and time constraints—interact to produce a tangled, chaotic web of instructional and personal problems. Moreover, the learning problems present in a classroom are often thought to be a result of a cyclical process in which home problems combine with seemingly random and uncontrollable forces present in the school setting to produce classroom problems of considerable magnitude. What results is a lack of learning and student and teacher dissatisfaction. This in turn produces other serious problems that affect motivation and behavior across environments.

The cyclical and complex nature of instructional problems is undeniable. Rarely is an instructional problem completely isolated from all other elements of the environment. Rather it is apparent that behaviors are shaped by environment, including physical conditions of the setting, values, and past experiences. This interaction between behavior and environment necessitates that instructional management be viewed from an ecological perspective. When viewed in this manner, instructional management becomes a task of carefully orchestrating diverse behavior and environmental variables to produce a setting that enhances and promotes learning.

An ecological perspective also recognizes that altering one element in an environment will produce corresponding changes in other elements of the environment. While these resultant changes may produce the desired result and eliminate the problem at hand, they may also cause a series of unanticipated consequences. Moving a child to the back of the classroom so that a youngster who is misbehaving may be seated near the teacher may, for example, have the desired and anticipated effect of alleviating a disruptive behavior problem. It may also, however, have the unexpected effect of producing learning difficulties and frustration if the student who was moved to the rear has an unnoticed hearing, vision, or attention deficit.

It seems clear that classrooms are not entities in which the physical conditions of the classroom and school, and the past experiences, behavior, and values of teachers and students, are carefully compartmentalized. In reality a classroom is a focal point for all of these variables. Home problems; learning difficulties; the attitudes of teachers, students, administrators, and parents; seating arrangements; lighting; room temperature; and instructional materials all influence the educational environment. Therefore, one of the first steps in effective instructional management is the comprehensive examination of the exact nature and interaction of all elements in the instructional environment.

ENVIRONMENTS THAT AFFECT THE INSTRUCTIONAL SETTING

The physiological, psychosocial, and physical environments exert a great influence upon the classroom environment. Moreover, these environments combine in novel ways to affect the behavior of students and teachers alike, thus making each classroom setting unique. This necessitates the analysis of the exact nature of each instructional setting.

This unique interaction of environments and behaviors explains the difference in the effectiveness of instructional settings. For example, some classrooms are quiet and well organized, while others are not so quiet and appear to be much more loosely organized. Regardless of this contrast, however, the same amount of learning may be taking place in both. On the other hand, there are similar classrooms in which there is little learning and a great deal of frustration. By examining the unique ecology of each setting, it is possible to identify and understand the specific variables related to successful instructional planning.

●●●

An Instructional Problem

James, a third-grader, had tested Ms. Williams' professional patience to the absolute limit. She had tried everything she knew to keep him in his seat and on-task during the morning reading and language arts lessons. She had restructured his work so as to make it more interesting, changed his seat so there would be fewer distractions, and given him extra attention and special notice for staying on-task—all to no avail. It seemed as if James was constantly out of his seat and fidgeting, and when he was on-task, he didn't appear to be concentrating on the task at hand.

One morning after a number of admonishments, Ms. Williams sent James to the principal's office. Through discussion, Mr. Norton, the principal, learned that lunch at school was the only meal that James consistently ate. In the morning, James was responsible for getting himself up and preparing breakfast if he was to receive any. In the afternoon, he came home to an empty house and a late dinner, if any at all. Mr. Norton realized that James had home problems that extended far beyond the provision of meals, but he also realized that a significant proportion of James' instructional problem involved simple hunger.

●●●

Physiological Environment

The physiological environment encompasses nutritional, health, and biophysical conditions. Children who are ill; who suffer from an inadequate diet, fatigue, allergies or physical impairments; or who are taking medication or consuming illicit drugs will not fully profit from the instructional program. While some of these elements of the physiological environment may be beyond the immediate control of the classroom teacher, they nevertheless must be successfully managed if learning is to take place.

It must also be remembered that the best attempts at implementing an instructional program will be thwarted unless the physiological environment is successfully managed. The most clever material and the best lesson will all be for naught if there is an unmanaged and significant physiological deficit.

● ●

An Instructional Problem

Math had always been hard for Howard. His mother constantly told him that he just didn't have a "math gene" and that he really shouldn't expect to be a good math student. Past experience had verified this. While Howard seemed to have a tenuous grasp of new concepts presented in class, he received little help or encouragement in completing his homework. This, added to the embarrassing experience of publicly displaying his ignorance when working problems on the blackboard, took a dramatic toll on Howard's motivation and self-concept.

Ms. Robbins, Howard's seventh-grade math teacher, recognized that Howard was slightly behind his peers in knowledge of math concepts, but his biggest problem was his expectation of failure. Ms. Robbins realized that her instructional program for Howard would have to involve some change in expectation on the part of Howard's mother, as well as a healthy dose of successful experiences for Howard.

● ●

Psychosocial Environment

The psychosocial environment includes values, expectations, emotions, past conditioning history, and interpersonal interactions. While many of these conditions are inferred from behavior, they nevertheless significantly affect how tasks are approached and events are evaluated. School performance may be affected, for example, if the values of children and parents are dramatically different from those expounded by teachers and school officials. Likewise, teachers, parents, and students can have unrealistic expectations of what should take place in the classroom or of each other's role in supporting the instructional program. There will undoubtedly be major problems if these expectations differ significantly or if they contribute to the development of an instructional program that is grossly inappropriate.

The instructional program is also affected by past student performance and interpersonal problems. Instructional plans for a high-achieving student in math, for example, would differ significantly from those constructed for a student with a long history of failure or an extremely serious parental or peer problem. As a result, while instructional planning has a lot to do with the presentation of material, it also is significantly affected by values, expectations, and motivation.

•••

An Instructional Problem

Michelle had always been a very eager learner. In the past, her work was always accurate, and its neatness reflected the sense of pride that most teachers try to instill. This year was different, however. Ms. Griggs' sixth-grade class was unstructured, and students were always wandering between learning centers. While most of the students seemed to thrive in this environment, it was deadly for Michelle. She couldn't stand the noise and constant movement, and she longed for her highly structured classes of previous years.

Fortunately, Ms. Griggs noticed that the learning environment in her class was not appropriate for Michelle. She realized that there really was no need to change the classroom system for most of the children but that a change was in order for Michelle. Through discussions with fellow teachers and school officials, Ms. Griggs was able to transfer Michelle to another sixth-grade class in which there was a great deal of structure.

•••

Physical Environment

The physical environment includes those things and objects used in daily living. In the home, this may include things such as books, televisions, radios, and household appliances and in the classroom, desks, instructional materials, lights, and heat. It is easy to see how elements of the physical environment affect behavior in the classroom. Reading, for example, is facilitated by readily available books, and math instruction is certainly made more clear with the use of manipulative objects. Classrooms that are colorful, nicely arranged, and have ample and appropriate instructional materials assist in establishing an environment that is conducive for learning and promotes teacher and student satisfaction.

The physical environment of the classroom is what is typically thought of when discussing instructional management. Materials, instructional groupings, the physical layout and condition of the room, and seating arrangements influence behavior and all must be carefully considered in instructional planning. These factors, however, constantly interact with elements of the psychosocial and physiological environments to produce instructional settings that have unique requirements. For example, a relatively unstructured large-group arrangement in which the students are required to use math skills to solve problems may be very appropriate for some students. But other students may actually find this setting aversive due to a lack of social or academic skills or personality conflicts with others in the group. For these students, it may be necessary to structure a much different program.

●●●

An Instructional Problem

Mr. Blair couldn't figure out exactly what was wrong with his instructional program. Everything seemed to be fine at the beginning of the year. He had assessed the children and developed an instructional plan that by all appearances seemed to be appropriate and relevant. The first several months were a delight: The students were learning, and everyone seemed satisfied. Slowly, however, things began to change. Now, the lessons seemed boring, the students unmotivated, and the assignments irrelevant.

After a particularly frustrating day, Mr. Blair realized that his students had been changing all year, but his instructional program had not. True, he presented the new material in the book, but his style, assignments, and instructional groupings had not changed. Worse yet, he had made no attempt to assess any of his students after that initial assessment. It was frightening. He didn't know when or how to change, but he knew something was not working.

●●●

ECOLOGICALLY ORIENTED INSTRUCTIONAL PLANNING

Instructional planning is a dynamic process. Behaviors and environments influence and interact to produce settings that are unique and ever changing. Therefore, a reading instructional program that was appropriate in September may not be appropriate in February.

The goal of instructional planning is to produce a classroom ecosystem that is stable, one in which there is a balance between all of the elements of diverse environments. This balance is very difficult to achieve and maintain due to constantly changing conditions. When the balance is lost, learning suffers, and education becomes burdensome.

Certainly, it is clear that if instructional planning is to to be effective, it must be realized that students are not all stamped out of the same mold. Each one is unique and constantly changing. Educational interventions, therefore, must be very carefully formulated so as to consider the effects upon all elements of the ecosystem. An intervention to change a child's values may, for example, have the desired classroom effect of producing a more compliant learner. The same intervention may also change the child's interaction in the home or community. This is not to argue against intervening. Rather, it is merely to note that interventions are complex and produce far-reaching changes in all elements of the ecosystem.

The realization of the complex nature of interventions is a necessary first step in instructional management. This understanding alone, however, is not sufficient. It must be accompanied by a comprehensive plan to continually assess specific targeted behaviors and conditions. This increases the probability that interventions will be appropriate, effective, and timely.

CHAPTER 2
DETECTING AND TARGETING PROBLEMS IN THE INSTRUCTIONAL SETTING

Targeting is the process of specifically defining and examining behaviors and environmental conditions, a critical element of any instructional intervention. Through the process of targeting, the ecological context of the behavior can be analyzed, thus allowing determination of the seriousness of the behavior, as well as other critical questions, such as:

Who is involved in the problem?
What environmental conditions are associated with the problem?
When does the problem occur?
Where does the problem occur?

Answers to these questions help define the limits of the problem and offer clues that may aid in developing an intervention.

TARGETING PROBLEMS

A necessary first step in the intervention process is to determine whether a serious problem exists. Not every classroom problem necessitates an intervention. Rather, the goal is to intervene only in those behaviors and conditions that have a serious and adverse effect on the instructional program. To do anything else wastes valuable time and energy that could be spent on more critical elements of the instructional program.

The effect that the instructional program has upon the teacher and student is perhaps the most critical factor in determining the existence of an instructional problem. When a student is not learning or is obviously dissatisfied with the instructional program, there is undoubtedly a serious problem. Likewise, a serious instructional problem may exist when a teacher is unhappy with the effectiveness or implementation of the educational program. The crucial question, of course, is how dissatisfied must a teacher be, or how much or how long must there be a lack of learning for there to be a problem?

Certainly, all teachers and students are at times less than pleased with the outcome of an educational program, and lulls in learning are to be expected. It is difficult, therefore, to place a time limit or specific degree of dissatisfaction on such problems, as they are situationally determined. In one classroom, for example, a teacher may be dissatisfied with an instructional program that is consistently producing student growth although not to the degree desired. Another teacher, however, may be quite pleased with exactly the same conditions and results. Additionally, while one teacher may be able to tolerate a lull in learning, another may not.

●●●

An Instructional Problem

Learning had turned into a random event in Mr. McNally's tenth-grade mathematics class. He knew that things were out of control. Everyday time just seemed to slip through his fingers. He was yelling too much and constantly warning students about rule infractions. Worst of all, the students weren't learning mathematics.

It was obvious even to Mr. McNally that the program was disorganized. He didn't have any clear-cut goals for the instructional program, homework was rarely turned in, he had stacks of ungraded papers on his desk, and frankly the program was boring. Increasingly, it seemed that his lessons came directly out of the book with little explanation of mathematical processes. There was no individualization of the curriculum, so some of the students were unchallenged while others had simply given up because they knew they wouldn't understand the material presented.

Mr. McNally knew the students were unmotivated (who would be motivated?), and he realized that he was developing an expectation of failure. He was a little apprehensive to realize that he was starting to dread coming to work. He knew that his students couldn't be happy either.

●●●

Critical Behaviors

The seriousness of an instructional problem is judged in relationship to what is expected or required for skill mastery. Research has shown, however, that a number of critical teacher and student behaviors, as well as classroom conditions, are associated with effective implementation of the instructional program. Chief among these are:

•Effort

Student: Is too much or too little effort spent completing tasks?

Teacher: Is too much or too little effort spent implementing the instructional program?

•Motivation

Student: Is sufficient and appropriate motivation provided to engage in and complete assigned tasks and behave in an expected manner?

Teacher: Is sufficient and appropriate motivation provided to conduct the instructional program?

•Time

Student: Is an appropriate amount of learning time available, and is it used efficiently?

Teacher: Is an organized and efficient plan in place for the use of classroom time?

•Expectations

Student: Does behavior in the classroom match school and teacher expectations?

Teacher: Are expectations concerning the student appropriate and positive?

•Organization

Student: Does the organization of the instructional program promote a maximum amount of learning?

Teacher: Is the instructional program organized in an appropriate and useable manner?

The answers to these questions help determine the vitality and appropriateness of an instructional program. Moreover, each of these variables results in some form of teacher or student behavior. When instructional problems occur, they are manifested in behavior and reflect deficits in one or more of these areas. When an instructional problem is suspected, therefore, it is absolutely critical that each of these variables be systematically examined in order to determine its foundation and nature. This analysis necessitates examining the amount as well as the severity of behavior.

The Amount of Behavior

The amount of behavior can be judged by:

frequency—the number of times the behavior occurs within a specified time period (Johnny hit Mary four times in 25 minutes)

latency—the length of time it takes for a behavior to occur once it has been prompted (the length of time it takes for Fred to start his math assignment after he has been told to start)

duration—the total length of time the behavior is performed (Joe was out of his seat for 6 minutes)

While it is not too difficult to judge the amount of behavior, it is more difficult to determine what amount should be expected. Violent behaviors, such as physical assault cannot be tolerated in any amount because it is extremely difficult to conduct the instructional program in the presence of such behaviors. Standards for less severe behaviors, such as talking-out, can be established by using peers to determine an acceptable range. For example, observation may indicate that students who are successful in the instructional program talk-out from 4 to 10 times each class period. It may be shown that this amount does not cause disruption in the instructional program and may serve as a standard by which to judge other students.

Behaviors can also be judged in relation to their functional use. For example, an examination of classroom behavior may indicate that a child can be out of his or her seat for no more than 8 of the 50 minutes during the class period and still perform adequately in the instructional program. This amount (8) may then serve as a standard by which to compare the performance of others. Likewise, for academic behaviors, it may be found that a specific rate of behavior is required for functional use. For example, a student who reads a passage at 60 words per minute may read so slowly as to preclude any possibility of functional skill use, while one who reads at 220 words a minute may be able to use and apply the skill with great ease.

The amount of critical teacher behaviors can be assessed in a similar manner. Behaviors, such as positive or negative teacher comments, the amount of time assigned to tasks, the number and timing of warnings, and the number and types of questions asked and assignments given, are controlled by the teacher and contribute significantly to the classroom environment. Unfortunately, it is often assumed that the problem in an instructional setting resides wholly within the student. As a result, a quest may be begun to assess and determine the exact amount of the student's problem. In truth, some of the problem may be due to student behavior; however, a certain amount also may be associated with teacher behavior, parental expectations, or environmental conditions in the school or home. Therefore, it is always a good rule to examine the amount of teacher as well as student behavior.

The Severity of Behavior

The severity of a behavior problem is best judged in a situation-specific manner. The ecology of each classroom is unique, as are the requirements for each instructional activity. What may be a problem in one setting may not be viewed as a problem in another. For example, while one teacher may judge missing a substantial number of problems on a worksheet an extremely serious problem, another may view the mistakes as learning opportunities and a chance to implement an instructional activity.

One of the key elements in this analysis is the determination of teacher tolerance of specific behaviors. Tolerance is affected by environmental conditions such as fatigue and the difficulty of activity. Everyone is less tolerant of behavior when feeling tired or ill, and oftentimes frustration and inappropriate behavior can be expected to occur when students attempt new and difficult tasks.

An analysis of the severity of behavior must also encompass an examination of the appropriateness of behavior to the setting, as well as the intent and magnitude of the response. Loud talking, for example, may be expected on the playground but not tolerated in the classroom during routine instruction. Likewise, a hit or a push that accidentally occurs during a game does not constitute a problem, while an intentional, aggressive assault may be judged to be quite severe.

It may be quite difficult to determine the exact degree of severity of a problem. Certainly, what at first glance appears to be an extremely severe problem often appears less serious several days later. Also, tolerance is constantly changing, such that behaviors that at one time were considered inappropriate for a setting are now permitted. Adding to this is the constant problem of trying to determine intent and magnitude.

The difficulty inherent in evaluating the severity of instructional and behavior problems points to the absolute necessity of a careful and thorough assessment of the entire environment of the student. The level of functional use of academic skills, teacher tolerance, perceptions of the severity of the problem by other professionals as well as the parents and student, and demands and expectations present in the setting all serve as standards against which the behavior problem is judged. While this judgement is far from exact, it does allow for examination of the degree of discrepancy between what is expected and what is actually happening.

From this comes a determination of the most serious problems necessitating intervention. For example, an analysis of a student's classroom behaviors may indicate that of numerous difficulties, wasting instructional time is the most severe in that it affects the student's acquisition of basic and prerequisite academic skills. In addition, it may be found that when off-task, the student bothers others and is developing a pattern of misconduct that extends into other classes.

Critical teacher behaviors must also be examined. Analysis of a problem may reveal that some teacher behaviors, as well as student behaviors, contribute to classroom difficulties. A derogatory comment made to a student about a failing or personal attribute, for example, is a serious act that could have a dramatic effect upon the student's educational environment. Clearly, it is important to remember to avoid pointing fingers or affixing blame. Rather, a careful analysis of the interaction between behavior and environment should be conducted, reviewing how interventions may affect both student and teacher.

● ●

An Instructional Problem

Shanna's mother, Ms. Walker, had just gotten her fourth phone call of the school year about her daughter's behavior in Ms. Drewry's class, and it was only October. Shanna, according to Ms. Drewry, wasn't finishing her work, was talking without permission, and "talked back" when corrected.

Ms. Walker took pride in her reputation as a cooperative parent, but totally exasperated, she asked Ms. Drewry just how much of a problem Shanna's behavior was. Ms. Drewry indicated that Shanna's failure to complete her work was an almost constant problem and was preventing her from adequately learning the material. The talking was a problem because it was annoying, but all of the students seemed to talk a lot; Shanna didn't talk any more than anyone else. Talking back was a worse problem. Although it didn't occur often, it was absolutely maddening when it did, and it helped create an environment that was not conducive for learning.

What came out of the discussion was a mutual realization that the talking really wasn't a big problem, but the infrequent episodes of talking back and the frequent failure to do homework were serious problems worthy of attention.

●●●

DEFINING PROBLEMS

An additional necessary step in the intervention process is development of a precise definition of the apparent problem and the conditions associated with it. Vague terms, such as hyperactive, unmotivated, and disorganized, may describe a constellation of conditions and behaviors. For example, hyperactivity may describe a child who constantly moves out of his or her seat, fails to complete work, and continually wanders around the room. On the other hand, this same term may be used by a teacher with a very low tolerance for classroom movement to describe a child who is an active yet eager learner. Likewise, caution must be taken in attributing problems to an internalized condition. Laziness or a lack of internal motivation, for example, may be said to be the reason for a child constantly failing to complete his or her work.

Explanations of this sort often ascribe problems to personality traits that are beyond the reach of any direct educational intervention. They therefore do little to assist in the development of interventions that can change the problems. A more appropriate approach would be to define changeable, observable, and measurable conditions in the environment—such as lack of relevant rewards, visual or auditory problems, or work that is too difficult—that may be associated with the problem.

●●●

An Instructional Problem

A multidisciplinary team had been assembled to try to determine the exact nature of Jerry's learning problem. The team consisted of a school psychologist, the school guidance counselor, Jerry's third-grade teacher, the special education teacher, Jerry's mother, and a local pediatrician.

At the initial meeting, it became apparent that Jerry was having a great deal of difficulty in the classroom. He wasn't completing his work and was frequently off-task; the work that was turned in was sloppy and inaccurate. This initial meeting resulted in the guidance counselor, who was serving as the chairperson, assigning various assessment tasks to each member of the team.

What resulted from these assessments was a rather confusing picture of a child. The pediatrician thought the problem was related to attention and rooted in a physiological disorder requiring medication. The school psychologist suggested that Jerry was learning disabled. The teachers didn't think Jerry was learning disabled but rather unmotivated. Jerry's mother didn't know what to think.

After listening to the occasionally strident debate for some time, the guidance counselor stated that the purpose of the assessments was not to put a label on Jerry but to determine the best way to teach him. What they had to do was concentrate on the specific conditions associated with Jerry's success and failure. This information, rather than a label, was basic in the development of an appropriate instructional program.

●●

USING A TEAM IN SELECTING TARGETS

Everyone involved in a classroom instructional problem has a perspective on the exact nature of the difficulty. Past experiences, social relationships, and professional expertise affect how problems are viewed and evaluated. As a result, parents, teachers, administrators, support staff, and students often have unique and divergent views of problem situations. A classroom teacher, for example, may relate a student's instructional problem to a lack of development of a prerequisite skill, while a school guidance counselor may believe that lack of motivation is the root of the problem. The parent, on the other hand, may fault the teacher's unrealistic expectations, and a pediatrician may link the problem to a physiological disorder requiring the administration of medication. What results from these very different views is recognition that a problem exists but little agreement as to its cause or exact nature.

It is very difficult to develop effective instructional plans when information is gathered only from one source or in one setting. Rather, effective ecological planning necessitates the comprehensive analysis of the behavior and perceptions of everyone associated with a problem setting, as well as the interactions that occur in various environments that may be associated with the classroom setting. For example, lack of time or place to do homework or various medical, peer, or parental problems may be the root of instructional difficulties. The teacher may not have information about these conditions, however, and may only see that an instructional difficulty is occurring in the classroom. Likewise, the parent may not understand that home conditions contribute to classroom difficulties, and the pediatrician may not have complete knowledge of what is and should be expected of the student or teacher at school.

All of this points to the necessity of using a team to identify targets for the instructional program. This team may consist of a special education teacher, regular education teacher, guidance counselor, psychologist, parent, social worker, school administrator, and health care professional. By using a team, a wide array of expertise can be focused on a problem, and certainly, a more complete view of the total ecology of the problem can be obtained.

Bringing together a variety of individuals, each with a somewhat different perspective, is not an easy task. Often disagreements as to the exact nature of the problem result in heated debates, culminating in accusation and placement of blame or failure on a particular institution or individual. This almost always results in a negative climate, obstructing implementation of effective intervention. A more reasonable approach is to try to seek agreement through collaboration, recognizing the unique perspective and skills of each individual and realizing that an effective plan may have to be multifaceted. When a team is used in this manner, an ecologically complete program is created—one that is thoroughly appropriate for all.

● ●

An Instructional Problem

Donna had always been an extremely good student, but her performance in seventh grade left a great deal to be desired. Language arts and math had always been fairly easy for her, and as a result she had been placed in honors sections of these courses. This year, however, Donna couldn't seem to keep up with the tremendous amount of homework that was assigned. In elementary school she had been able to keep up with her homework and still participate in all of the extracurricular activities that she enjoyed. This year it was a different story: She just couldn't get everything done.

Donna found that the classes were noisy, there didn't seem to be any organization, and the teachers covered new and increasingly more difficult material far too fast for her to comprehend. Because they were in honors classes, the teacher expected all of the students to function independently with few instructions. This was disastrous for Donna. Her performance declined significantly. She began feigning illness to avoid class, cried over homework, and when she came to class was unprepared and dreaded participating.

Ms. Hart, the school counselor, realized that Donna was facing some very real problems and that unless they were addressed comprehensively and quickly, they would escalate. What was clear was that Donna was not learning and that she and her teachers were extremely unhappy about the entire situation. It was also clear to Ms. Hart that all of the problems were connected and that any instructional intervention had to target a number of areas.

• •

SELECTING TARGETS

As previously stated, lack of effort or motivation, inefficient use of time, unrealistic or inappropriate expectations, poor organization, and lack of student learning indicate that serious instructional problems exist. Certainly, each of these areas of the instructional setting must be carefully examined. In addition, however, this examination should include the ecological setting of the problem to determine specific environmental conditions and behaviors that may be contributory. Listed in Table 2-1 are variables in the physiological, physical, and psychosocial environments that can affect the effectiveness of an instructional setting.

TABLE 2.1 Targeting Environmental Conditions

Variables in the Physiological Environment

Health Factors:
    illness
    allergy
    fatigue
    diet
    exercise
Physical Impairments:
    sensory loss (e.g., vision, hearing)
    orthopedic and neurological impairments (e.g., cerebral palsy)
Drugs or Medication:
    prescribed medications
    alcohol
    illicit drugs

TABLE 2.1 Targeting Environmental Conditions (continued)

Variables in the Physical Environment

Resources or Conditions in the Home and Community:
 housing
 basic needs (e.g., clothing)
 parental supervision
 home routine
 methods of discipline
 significant events (e.g., divorce)
 community resources (e.g., recreation)
School Factors:
 roles of administrators, teachers, and staff
 curricula design
 school routine (e.g., order, structure)
 physical facility and classroom materials (e.g., texts, workbooks)
 community involvement
Classroom Arrangements:
 physical properties of classroom (e.g., noise, temperature, room color)
 classroom density (e.g., crowding)
Classroom and Instructional Factors:
 learning climate (e.g., structure, organization, positive rules)
 curriculum and instructional materials
 program delivery (e.g., diversity of tasks, engaged time, instructional arrangements, instructional techniques)

Variables in the Psychological and Social Environment

Emotional and Learning Impairments:
 emotional impairments
 mental retardation
 learning disabilities
 communication disorders

Interpersonal Factors
 effects of the behavior of teachers, parents, peers, others

Intrapersonal Factors:
 interests
 values
 motivation
 expectations

Source: From *Behavior and instructional management* (p. 39), by W. H. Evans, S. S. Evans, and R. E. Schmid (Boston: Allyn and Bacon, 1989). Copyright © 1989 by Allyn and Bacon. Reprinted by permission.

TABLE 2.2   Behavior Network

INAPPROPRIATE BEHAVIORS	APPROPRIATE BEHAVIORS
Begins tasks after being reminded	Begins task promptly
Does not attend to tasks	Attends to tasks
Fails to complete tasks	Completes tasks
Does not follow directions	Follows directions
Does careless or sloppy work	Completes neat work
Is out-of-seat	Remains in-seat
Interrupts others	Speaks at appropriate times
Talks-out	Talks with permission
Does not tell the truth	Tells the truth
Uses abusive language	Uses appropriate language
Tattles	Reports events accurately
Withdraws from others	Interacts with others
Requests constant reassurance	Participates without constant reassurance
Makes self-deprecating statements	Makes realistic statements about self
Cries at inappropriate times	Cries at appropriate times
Engages in inappropriate age play	Engages in appropriate age play
Fails to initiate contact with others	Initiates contact with others
Fails to engage in group activities	Initiates contact with group
Gives up easily	Is persistent
Refuses to share with others	Shares with others
Personal mood does not fit setting	Personal mood fits setting

TABLE 2.2 Behavior Network (continued)

INAPPROPRIATE BEHAVIORS	APPROPRIATE BEHAVIORS
Claims illness without apparent physical cause	Claims illness with apparent physical cause
Shuns responsibility for behaviors	Accepts responsibility for behaviors
Is uncooperative	Is cooperative
Disobeys class and school rules	Follows class and school rules
Is assaultive	Resolves problems without violence
Destroys property	Respects property
Exhibits temper in solving problems	Resolves problems appropriately
Steals	Uses things with permission
Cheats	Completes own work

Source: Adapted from S. S. Evans, W. H. Evans, and C. D. Mercer, *Assessment for Instruction.* Copyright © 1986 by Allyn and Bacon. Reprinted by permission.

Problems are situationally defined. Therefore, targeting seeks to find unique ways in which each variable contributes to educational success and failure. This allows development of an educational plan that meets the specific needs of each student.

Classroom behaviors may also be targeted for intervention. Listed in Table 2-2 are student behaviors that can be severely disruptive to the instructional program. It is important to remember that the thrust of any intervention is not simply to stop a behavior but rather change it into an appropriate behavior. Thus, appropriate companion behaviors are listed in this table. Targeting therefore becomes the process of identifying not only what needs to be decreased but also what needs to be increased.

CHAPTER 3
ASSESSING BEHAVIORS AND SETTING GOALS

Assessment in many regular education classrooms is often thought of as a formal process in which a standardized test is administered to students at each grade level in order to determine relative academic standing. In special education classrooms, assessment is often thought of as a necessary administrative evil in which standardized tests are administered to students at the beginning and end of each school year in order to initiate and end an Individualized Educational Program (IEP). The assessment information gathered for these purposes may be interesting but incomplete and somewhat irrelevant for the purpose of instructional planning.

In fact, the unique needs of each setting and student cannot be detected adequately by the periodic use of tests that are largely designed to illustrate how the student's performance compares to that of his or her agemates. Rather, what is needed is an assessment process that can be used continuously and comfortably to assess student learning and detect significant and subtle changes in performance. When used in this manner, assessment will directly lead to the correction of instructional difficulties.

TYPES OF ASSESSMENT INSTRUMENTS

Assessment instruments fall into one of two categories:

1. *Norm-referenced assessment* instruments are administered in a specific or standardized manner. The student's assessment results are compared to those of a normative group, allowing determination of relative standing, such as by grade or age achievement level or percentile. Instruments of this type are not designed to comprehensively assess each behavior or instructional skill to which the student may be exposed but rather sample selected behaviors or skills at each grade or age level.
2. In *criterion-referenced assessment*, the student is not compared to others but to a criterion level that reflects a desired level of performance. Often the student's performance and criterion are expressed as a percentage or rate of correct or appropriate responses or successful trials.

Teacher-made tests are a common form of criterion-referenced measurement. Instructional materials are used to comprehensively assess each learning objective in the curriculum. Flashcards, worksheets, manipulatives, and oral reading material are but some examples of the materials. As is true with other types of criterion-referenced assessment, specific error patterns can be noted and the student's responses compared to a criterion of achievement often expressed as percentage correct or rate per minute. The data from these instruments may be very relevant in educational programming in that they allow an examination of the student's response to actual instructional materials and conditions. Further information on teacher-made tests in specific academic subject areas is presented in other texts in the *Detecting and Correcting* series.

●●

An Instructional Problem

Ms. Jones noticed that Jennifer, a fourth-grader, read slowly and with great difficulty. She referred Jennifer to the school's reading specialist, who administered a standardized, norm-referenced test, which revealed that Jennifer's oral reading and word identification skills were at the second-grade level. These data provided compelling evidence to Ms. Jones and Jennifer's parents that a reading problem did exist. This information by itself, however, was not complete and did not suggest an appropriate remedial strategy.

To develop an instructional program, the reading specialist gave Jennifer a criterion-referenced test that the teachers in the school had developed using instructional materials from the school's basal reading program. This test indicated that Jennifer had mastered only 30% of the fourth-grade vocabulary words, 50% of the third-grade words, and 85% of the second-grade words. In addition, Jennifer had a particular phonetic pattern of errors, and while her reading rate was acceptable on high-second-grade/low-third-grade work, it was unacceptably low on fourth-grade material.

Ms. Jones used the information from the criterion-referenced test to develop an instructional program that addressed Jennifer's particular problems and assigned her an oral reader at an appropriate level of difficulty. Ms. Jones did this with some assurance that the intervention was needed and appropriate.

●●

It is important to recognize that one type of assessment is not necessarily superior to another. Each type of assessment has a slightly different function and use in instructional planning. Norm-referenced tests are used to show relative standing but do little to show the degree to which a student has learned a specific series of skills. Conversely, it is quite difficult to form a normative comparison by using a criterion-referenced test. Criterion-referenced tests, however, are extremely useful in detecting specific instructional strengths and weaknesses and the extent to which a skill has been acquired.

The lesson to be learned from this is that it is essential first to determine the function of assessment. This will enhance selection of appropriate assessment instruments.

ASSESSMENT GUIDELINES

Data collection is a tool to be used in detecting and correcting instructional problems. Information concerning student performance can guide the teacher in developing and implementing the instructional program and make learning much more efficient and enjoyable. It is possible, however, to collect irrelevant data or to make the process cumbersome, tedious, or overcomplicated. When this occurs data collection will actually impede the most important function of the teacher—teaching. The following guidelines will assist in eliminating this problem:

1. *Collect only relevant and accurate data.* Students' cumulative folders provide an illustration of the tremendous amounts of data that can be collected concerning student performance. These folders often contain copious quantities of information concerning the student's health and family life, anecdotal comments from past teachers that address the student's classroom performance, past grades, discipline reports, results of achievement and intelligence assessment, observational data, and so on. Not all of this information is needed for every intervention. In addition, some of the information is highly subjective. For instance, opinions of past teachers may inaccurately detail the amount and nature of the student's behavior, thus leading to unwarranted conclusions.

     Assessing noncritical areas wastes the time and effort of both teachers and students. Additionally, inaccurate information may lead to developing educational programs that are grossly inappropriate.
2. *Assess the environment, not just the student.* In school settings, it is often assumed that an intrinsic quality or behavior of the student is the sole cause of a problem. While the student's behavior may be very inappropriate, it must always be understood in an ecological context.

That is to say that the behavior of others, as well as environmental conditions, must be carefully considered. It is certainly inappropriate for a student to throw instructional materials on the floor; however, the evaluation of this behavior may, for example, indicate that the student was sick, the instructional materials too difficult, or that the episode was preceded by a sarcastic remark.

In correcting instructional problems, it is not sufficient to know only that a behavior is inappropriate. It is more important to know what unique behavior and environmental conditions preceded and followed the behavior. Once these ecological variables have been detected, it is possible to develop an individualized instructional program that will correct the specific causes of the behavior or instructional difficulties.

3. *Keep data collection simple.* Data collection can be extremely cumbersome and consume a tremendous amount of time. When data collection becomes overly complicated, it actually interferes with teaching. Therefore, a cardinal rule of assessment is to keep the procedures simple and report the results in a straightforward manner.

4. *Assess learning as well as performance.* A one-time assessment will provide information concerning student performance. Learning is assessed by measuring performance over time. While performance assessment is important, it will not demonstrate trends or daily changes in student performance. To detect these changes, data must be collected frequently, such as on a daily basis. Frequent analysis allows for examination of the extent and direction of learning so that subtle changes in student performance can be easily detected. This information allows interventions to be applied in a timely and appropriate manner.

●●●

An Instructional Problem

It was only three weeks into the school year, but it seemed like months. Mr. Jones, a seventh-grade social studies teacher, was tired and frustrated, due primarily to Anthony, who seemed never to pay attention, always bothered others, and forever asked irrelevant questions.

A quick review of Anthony's cumulative folder provided a running narrative of past teacher complaints about his lack of attention and misbehavior. A closer reading revealed, however, that Anthony rarely misbehaved in math classes in which he was given discrete assignments that could be completed in a quiet setting. One previous teacher in fact noted that Anthony was an active and valuable member of an instructional group when given clearly defined rules and able to apply the information obtained from his assignments.

Mr. Jones developed an instructional program for Anthony that utilized this information. In addition, Mr. Jones kept a daily log of Anthony's most annoying behaviors, the number of times he bothered others, and the number and accuracy of completed homework assignments. To Mr. Jones' delight, the intervention was effective, and there was a dramatic improvement in Anthony's classroom behavior and performance in social studies.

•••

SOURCES OF ASSESSMENT DATA

In assessing instructional problems, it is critical to obtain information from a wide variety of people in numerous settings. An ecological assessment requires input from a team consisting of the student, teachers, parents, peers, and social and health care workers. Such an assessment fully examines the entire environment of the student and how behaviors and conditions interact. A more limited assessment may miss a great deal of relevant information and lead to development of an instructional program that is inappropriate. As displayed in Table 3-1, a wide variety of information can be obtained from numerous sources.

DATA COLLECTION FOR ECOLOGICAL ASSESSMENT

Data collection has many uses in education. Initially, data are collected for the purposes of detecting instructional problems and selecting targets for interventions. These and additional data may be used to formulate an instructional program. Following this, ongoing data may be gathered to further refine and readjust programs to meet the changing needs of the student and environment. Clearly, assessment is a dynamic process in which numerous people continually contribute a variety of information from diverse environments.

An ecological assessment must evaluate behavior, as well as how people perceive instructional problems. An evaluation without each of these components is incomplete and can lead to inappropriate targets and interventions.

TABLE 3.1   Sources of Assessment Data

POSSIBLE SOURCES OF INFORMATION	INFORMATION THAT MAY BE OBTAINED
Student	Current behavior in school, community, home Interaction with others Academic and social skills and abilities Expectations, values, attitudes Learning environment information (classroom and instructional factors)
Peers	Expectations and values Interaction with students Activities student and peers engage in
Teachers and School Personnel	Past and current behavior and academic performance Skills and abilities of student Learning environment information (classroom and instructional factors) Expectations and values
Parents	Home conditions and resources Expectations, values, interaction between family members Health information Past and current behavior of student
Health Care Personnel	Health information
Social Agency Workers	Agencies involved and services received by student
School Records	Past attendance Prior retentions Past grades, behavior, discipline records Health information Measures of abilities and skills Special services and programs Learning environment information (classroom and instructional factors) Home factors

Source: From *Behavior and instructional management* (p. 67), by W. H. Evans, S. S. Evans, and R. E. Schmid (Boston: Allyn and Bacon, 1989). Copyright © 1989 by Allyn and Bacon. Reprinted by permission.

Assessment of Perceptions

In any assessment it is important to realize that there may be a difference between people's perceptions of behavior and the actual behavior, for these perceptions will dictate how behavior is evaluated. While perceptions may be quite accurate, they may also be affected by past experience or expectations about a student. A teacher may, for example, believe that a particular student's behavior is inappropriate and quite different from that of his or her peers. But further examination may indicate that the student's behavior does not differ substantially from that of classmates and is not really inappropriate when considering his or her age. A teacher may also have unrealistic expectations or fail to recognize that a student is experiencing severe instructional difficulties. Likewise, students and parents may have inaccurate perceptions of school or the behavior of the teacher.

This is not to say that opinion should not be considered, quite the contrary. Rather, it is important to realize that everyone, including teachers, parents, and students, has beliefs that are affected by past experience and preferences. These perceptions affect how behavior and conditions are evaluated. They may be accurate or inaccurate; nevertheless, they must be considered in any assessment. A variety of procedures can be used to assess perceptions:

1. *Checklists and rating scales.* On a checklist, the rater is asked to answer yes or no to a series of statements about a behavior or condition. A rating scale is very similar but differs in that the rater may respond to each question on a scale (such as 1–5) that indicates the degree of occurrence or severity. Although similar behaviors may be considered, the format and specificity of information may differ, as can be seen in these examples of checklist and rating scale items:

   Checklist Items

   Teacher Checklist
   - The student always begins work promptly.   (yes/no)
   - The student is frequently out-of-seat.   (yes/no)

   Student Checklist
   - The teacher always explains the work.   (yes/no)
   - I generally enjoy math class.   (yes/no)

   Parent Checklist
   - My child generally understands his or her
     homework.   (yes/no)
   - My child enjoys going to school.   (yes/no)

Rating Scale Items

1 = never   2 = rarely   3 = sometimes   4 = often   5 = always

Teacher Rating Scale
- The student begins work promptly.   1 2 3 4 5
- The student is out-of-seat.   1 2 3 4 5

Student Rating Scale
- The teacher explains the work.   1 2 3 4 5
- I enjoy math class.   1 2 3 4 5

Parent Rating Scale
- My child understands his or her homework.   1 2 3 4 5
- My child enjoys going to school.   1 2 3 4 5

Generally, there should be 30 or less items on a checklist or rating scale, and they should reflect the most important elements of the instructional problem being investigated. In addition, the person completing the checklist or rating scale should have knowledge of the variable being assessed. The teacher, for example, may have little direct knowledge of conditions in the home; likewise, the parent may not know exactly what conditions exist in the classroom.

2. *Interviews.* An interview may be written or oral. Regardless of the form, the person conducting the interview should have a clear idea of what is to be accomplished and should prepare open-ended questions that encourage elaboration. This will eliminate the possibility of the interview drifting into extraneous topics.

Interviews can be used to provide clarification of responses obtained from checklists or rating scales. It is critical, however, that the interviewer be nonjudgmental and provide ample opportunity for the person being interviewed to fully express his or her opinions.

Written interviews may consist of autobiographies, essays, or specific items that would normally be asked in an oral interview. Written interviews have the advantage of allowing the person to carefully formulate a response. They have the disadvantage of eliminating a face-to-face meeting and being dependent upon the individual's skills in reading and writing. Examples of questions that may be asked in an oral interview include:

Student Interview Items
- What do you enjoy most at school?
- What do you dislike most about school?
- Suggest four ways to help you improve your behavior.

Parent Interview Items
- What types of reading materials does Kyle enjoy at home?
- How is discipline handled at home?
- Describe homework assignments that are easy for Lindsey.

●●

An Instructional Problem

Ms. Harrison, the guidance counselor, had been asked by the principal to observe Cindy's behavior in school. A rating scale that had been completed by Cindy's third-grade teacher indicated that Cindy was frequently off-task and talked-out far too much in class. Classroom observations, however, did not suggest that Cindy talked-out or was off-task more than her peers. Ms. Harrison did note that Cindy periodically threw back her head and talked quietly to herself, but this was always followed by Cindy's return to the assigned task.

Ms. Harrison's subsequent interviews with Cindy and her teacher revealed that each had strongly held opinions of the other. Cindy's teacher believed that Cindy's behavior was unusual and indicative of a problem. Cindy, for her part, believed that the teacher was unfair and picked on her. Ms. Harrison concluded that, while some of Cindy's behavior was a little out of the ordinary, the larger problem was the inaccurate perceptions that Cindy and her teacher held for each other.

●●

Assessment of Behaviors

An analysis of the amount and nature of behavior must also be considered in an ecological assessment. This assessment should be designed to measure the effect that various environmental variables have upon behavior. For example, while it is helpful to know that 20 talk-outs occurred in a 50-minute class period, it is more useful to know which specific environmental conditions were related to the talk-outs. This information is vital in formulating educational programs that can be used in correcting instructional problems.

Several elements of behavior can be observed:

1. *Frequency*—the number of times that a behavior occurs within a specified period of time (i.e., 10 hits in 5 minutes = 2 per minute).
2. *Duration*—the total length of time the behavior occurs (i.e., out-of-seat for 6 total minutes).
3. *Latency*—the time between when the behavior is prompted and when it begins (i.e., It took Johnny 3 minutes to start his work after Ms. Smith told him to begin).
4. *Topography*—the form of the behavior (i.e., Frances was sitting backward in her chair).
5. *Magnitude*—the force of the behavior (i.e., Vivian threw the pencil with such force that it stuck into the bulletin board).

Before observing a behavior, it is necessary first to determine which of these elements of behavior is to be observed. Sometimes the nature of the behavior dictates the selection. For example, it is probably more practical to observe the frequency and magnitude of hits rather than their duration. Likewise, the duration of being off-task may be more important than the frequency.

When conducting an observation, the observer should:

• be as unobtrusive as possible
• observe appropriate as well as inappropriate behavior
• immediately record the data
• identify events that cause or are related to behaviors
• observe for as long as possible

Following these guidelines will increase the probability that the data collected will be accurate and reflect the unique needs of the student and nature of the setting.

There are several methods of recording observational data. The method selected will reflect the element of behavior that is of greatest concern.

1. *Event recording.* Each occurrence of a behavior is recorded. As displayed in Table 3-2, for example, the number and types of oral reading errors may be recorded.
2. *Duration and latency recording.* Record is made of the time at which a behavior was prompted and the time at which it started. The latency of the behavior can then be determined. For example, Ms. Jones asked Freddy to start his math assignment at 9:00. Freddy did not start his assignment, however, until 9:08. This means that there was an 8-minute latency.

    Duration recording is accomplished in much the same fashion, recording the beginning and ending times of the behavior. For

TABLE 3.2   Event Recording of Reading Errors

NAME: Lindsey
Behavior: Oral reading errors
Observation Time: 10:00–10:30

TYPE OF ERRORS	NUMBER OF ERRORS	TOTAL NUMBER OF ERRORS
Ommissions	////	4
Repetitions	//	2
Unknown or aided	⊔⊓⊤ /	6
Self-corrected	/	1
Substitutions		0
Mispronunciations	//	2
Reversals	/	1
Hesitations		0

example, Ashley got out of her seat at 10:15 and did not sit down again until 10:25, a duration of 10 minutes.

3. *Permanent product recording.* The tangible evidence of student behavior, such as completed math problems or correct spelling words, is recorded. Number or percentage of correct or incorrect responses can be tallied on a daily basis and recorded on a chart that illustrates student growth.

This type of recording procedure is very useful and practical in educational settings in that the teacher does not have to be present for each occurrence of the behavior. Rather, the teacher can collect worksamples and evaluate them at a later time, as is the case with homework. This allows the teacher more time to conduct classroom instructional activities. Worksheets, tape recordings of oral readings, and written classroom assignments are but some examples of permanent product recording.

Care must be taken with this type of recording system in determining authorship. There is always the possibility that someone other than the student completed the assignment. Additionally, when an error occurs it is extremely difficult to determine the exact process that the student went through in completing the problem. As a result, it may be difficult to develop a program that remediates the student's specific weakness or error pattern.

4. *Anecdotal recording.* A written record is made of antecedent events (those events that occur before behavior) and consequent events (those events that occur after behavior), and their relationship to specific behaviors. As illustrated in Table 3-3, a specific pattern of

TABLE 3.3   Antecedent and Consequent Anecdotal Record Form

NAME: Tommy
Behavior: Refuses to start classroom assignment
Observation Time: 8:50—9:40

ANTECEDENT	BEHAVIOR	CONSEQUENT
Teacher told students to go to their math learning centers	Sat in seat and stated that he would not participate	Teacher talked to Tommy about importance of following teacher instructions
Teacher asked Tommy to get his math worksheet	Failed to comply	Teacher brought worksheet to Tommy
Teacher asked Tommy to correct missed problems on worksheet	Stated that he was bored and was not going to make corrections	Teacher said that it was Tommy's decision and that it was okay this time not to correct problems
Teacher asked Tommy to return to his seat for language arts lesson	Remained out-of-seat	Teacher reminded Tommy of rules four times and then told him he could sit in any seat if he would just sit

environmental events is related to Tommy's refusal to engage in classroom assignments.

Anecdotal recording has several advantages. First, it allows the observer to provide specific details about the topography of a behavior. For example, it may be difficult to determine why a teacher would be upset over a student raising his or her hand in a classroom unless accompanied by the anecdotal report of associated behaviors of yelling and grunting. Second and perhaps more important, anecdotal recording allows a thorough examination of the specific elements of the environment related to behavior. This information is essential in detecting and correcting instructional problems. In fact, without it, it is virtually impossible to design an educational program that will effectively meet the needs of the student and setting.

Charting Data

Most observational data is best illustrated on a chart. A chart should have a horizontal axis, illustrating time such as days or weeks, and a vertical axis, showing the amount of behavior such as time of duration or latency, frequency, number correct or incorrect, or percentage. Two

FIGURE 3.1   Interval and Bar Charts

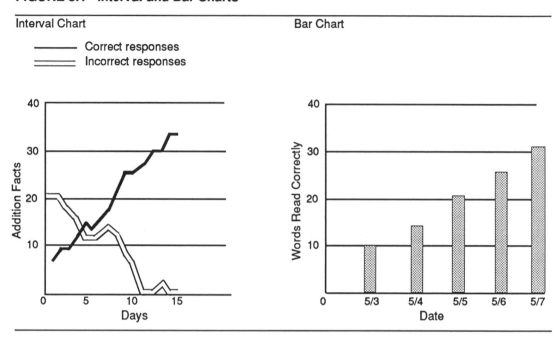

of the most common types of charts, an equal interval chart and a bar chart, are presented in Figure 3-1.

GOAL SETTING

All too often interventions are designed to fix or change a student's behavior. While at times this is an appropriate goal, it must be remembered that other elements of the environment may also need to change. Therefore, a comprehensive analysis of the entire environment must be conducted before establishing intervention goals.

Goals for Perceptions

As illustrated in Table 3-4, assessment data may indicate that the problem involves perception as well as behavior. Clearly, no intervention is needed when perceptions are positive and behavior is appropriate. When that is not the case, however, the goal of an intervention must be multifaceted and address perception as well as behavior. As a result, goal setting involves changing the perception to match the behavior, while in other cases, the goal is to make the perception more accurate or reflect a realistic and desirable standard of behavior. To change behavior

TABLE 3.4 Assessment Outcomes and Possible Interventions

ASSESSMENT OUTCOMES	POSSIBLE INTERVENTIONS
1. Perception—Positive Behavior—Appropriate	The perceptions and behavior match. No intervention is necessary
2. Perception—Positive Behavior—Inappropriate	The perceptions and behaviors don't match. An intervention may be needed to make the perceptions more accurate and improve behavior.
3. Perception—Negative Behavior—Appropriate	The perceptions and behaviors don't match. An intervention may be needed to change perceptions.
4. Perception—Negative Behavior—Inappropriate	The perceptions and behavior match. Interventions may be needed to change perceptions and improve behavior.

Source: From *Behavior and instructional management* (p. 96), by W. H. Evans, S. S. Evans, and R. E. Schmid (Boston: Allyn and Bacon, 1989). Reprinted by permission.

without changing the attitude about the behaver is inefficient and ineffective. Likewise, attempting to change an attitude without addressing the behavior is ill advised.

Perceptions can be measured by the use of rating scales and checklists. In addition, the behavior associated with a perception can also be observed. Teachers often, for example, respond differently to students about whom they have negative expectations. In this sense, teachers are not different from anyone else.

Goals for Behavior

Establishing a terminal or final goal for a behavior is an extremely crucial decision: If it is too low, the student may become disinterested and unchallenged. If it is too high, the student may become unnecessarily frustrated. Goals for most social behaviors—such as the amount of time on-task, the number of talk-outs, and the number of interactions with peers—are situationally determined. That is, the goal changes with the requirements of the setting. For example, four talk-outs per period may be considered acceptable in a class in which the teacher has a high tolerance for talk-outs and the instructional setting encourages spontaneous discourse. In a class in which silence is the rule, four talk-outs would be an inappropriately high goal.

Terminal goals may also be established in relation to the requirements for successful usage of the behavior. For example, observation of

FIGURE 3.2 Daily Goals

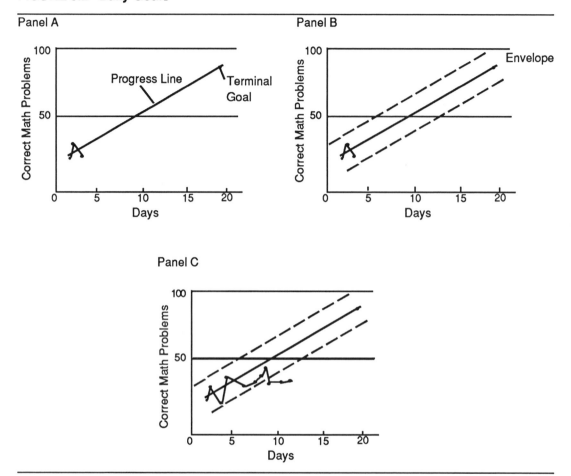

successful student interaction in the workplace, classroom, or home may indicate that a specific rate or amount of behavior should be required. Likewise, data collected from academically competent students can be used as a goal. In a second-grade math class, for example, the rate at which academically successful students say their addition facts could serve as a goal for that particular skill.

A great deal of data collected by several precision teaching projects indicate that certain response rates on academic tasks are related to improved performance on subsequent, more difficult tasks. Seeing/saying words in a list (80+ per minute), oral reading of text (150–200 words per minute), and seeing/writing math facts (55–75 digits per minute) are but a few examples of these rates.

While terminal goals are important, the success of an instructional program is dependent upon daily or short-term goals. Through achieving daily goals, the student is able to approach and eventually reach the final goal. Additionally, daily goals clearly illustrate what is required of the student and allow daily analysis of performance. As a result, deviations in performance can be quickly noted and interventions applied in a timely manner.

One of the best ways of establishing daily goals is illustrated in Figure 3-2. As displayed in Panel A, an estimated progress line is drawn from the midpoint of several days of initial data to a final goal. This line represents the desired daily goal. In all probability, however, the student's daily performance will not fall exactly on the line. Therefore, as illustrated in Panel B, an envelope can be drawn around the progress line, providing an acceptable and achievable daily goal. The envelope can be widened to ensure daily success or narrowed to create a more challenging environment.

An instructional problem can be detected when the student's responses fall outside the envelope for a predetermined number of consecutive days. As illustrated in Panel C of Figure 3-2, progress is adequate during the first 8 days of instruction. The data for days 9 through 11, however, fall outside the envelope and indicate an instructional problem necessitating intervention.

Instructional problems can also be detected by analyzing the trend of student performance. Common data trends and instructional decisions are presented in Figure 3-3 on pages 40 and 41.

● ●

An Instructional Problem

Mr. Wilson's goal as an elementary special education teacher was to mainstream students whenever possible. In Mr. Wilson's opinion Terry was ready to go back into his regular fifth-grade classroom. The problem was that the fifth-grade teacher, Ms. Hardy, was convinced that returning Terry to the class would prompt more of the chaos that initiated his removal.

Rather than create a confrontation between himself and Ms. Hardy, Mr. Wilson patiently listened to Ms. Hardy's concerns and detailed the program that he had successfully implemented with Terry. The daily data he had collected helped paint a picture of a student whose problems had been successfully addressed. After a great deal of discussion, Ms. Hardy agreed to work cooperatively with Mr. Wilson in establishing a program to return Terry to his regular classroom.

FIGURE 3.3 Common Data Trends

SINGLE DATA TRENDS

The amount of behavior is increasing. If the change is desired, no intervention is necessary. If the change is not desired, an intervention may be necessary.

The amount of behavior is decreasing. If the change is desired, no intervention is necessary. If the change is not desired, an intervention may be necessary.

The amount of behavior has become stable. If the goal has been reached, a new skill or behavior may be introduced. If the goal has not been reached, an intervention may be necessary to increase performance.

TRENDS FOR CORRECT AND INCORRECT OR APPROPRIATE AND INAPPROPRIATE RESPONSES

● — correct, or appropriate, responses
□ — incorrect, or inappropriate, responses

Both responses are worsening. An intervention is necessary.

Correct, or appropriate, responses are increasing, but so are the incorrect, or inappropriate, responses. An intervention may be necessary to decrease the incorrect, or inappropriate, responses.

Incorrect, or inappropriate, responses are decreasing, but so are the correct, or appropriate, responses. An intervention may be necessary to increase the correct, or appropriate, responses.

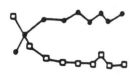

Both responses have become stable. If the goals have been reached, a new skill or behavior may be introduced. If the goals have not been reached, an intervention may be necessary to increase correct, or appropriate, responses and decrease incorrect, or inappropriate, responses.

FIGURE 3.3 Common Data Trends (continued)

TRENDS FOR CORRECT AND INCORRECT OR
APPROPRIATE AND INAPPROPRIATE RESPONSES (continued)

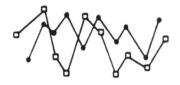

There is great variability in the data. The definition of the responses and recording procedures should be examined. A further examination may be necessary to identify the causes of the variability.

The data indicate that growth is occurring. No change is needed.

Source: From *Behavior and instructional management* (pp. 98–99), by W. H. Evans, S. S. Evans, and R. E. Schmid (Boston: Allyn and Bacon, 1989). Reprinted by permission.

The program that was agreed upon required Ms. Hardy to select several of Terry's behaviors that she felt should be decreased or increased. This required reflection and observation of Terry's peers to establish realistic goals. Ms. Hardy and Mr. Wilson shared this information with Terry and developed a chart that illustrated a final goal and daily goals. It was agreed that Terry could record his own data, with Ms. Hardy spot checking, and that a time at the end of the day would be established for Ms. Hardy and Terry to talk about and record his daily progress.

The program was a complete success. Mr. Wilson noted that Ms. Hardy's perception of Terry had changed and that Terry was able to fully profit from the educational program.

●●●

REFLECTIONS

1. The organization of Part I underscores that detecting special needs involves addressing individual as well as environmental variables. List the important variables that may influence behavior, and categorize each as an individual versus environmental factor.

2. Many of the difficulties students have in school are actually linked to circumstances outside the classroom. Identify at least five of the most important factors.

3. Behavior can be viewed according to both quantitative and qualitative dimensions. What are some of these dimensions? Why is it useful to take both dimensions into account?

4. Teacher assessment should be guided by knowledge of various aspects of the teaching and learning processes. List four assumptions that help guide decisions about classroom assessment.

5. Ecological assessment is not a singular, isolated event; rather, it examines a complete picture of student-environmental elements that contribute to target selection and intervention. What major steps would you take to conduct an ecological assessment of a behavior problem?

6. In establishing terminal goals of behavior, a range of issues must be considered. List the factors that influence a specific academic skill and then a particular social skill.

7. Review the strategies suggested for assessing behavior. Keep a written account of each step so that you can more easily make changes, refine the process, and finally repeat it successfully in the future.

8. Observe a student in elementary school, another in middle school, and one in high school who are experiencing problems; identify at least five possible behavior and environmental targets for each. After selecting these targets, interview the student's teachers and if possible parents or guardians to determine their opinions of possible targets. Compare and contrast the information.

9. Conduct an ecological assessment of the various environments for each of the students selected in question 8. List the factors found in each environment that may influence the problem setting. Describe how the assessment process and factors assessed change in relation to the age of the student.

10. In addition to the information presented in Chapters 1, 2, and 3, consult psychology and other special education textbooks and journals that address management problems. Compare information in these chapters with that found in the following sources:

Alberto, P. A., & Troutman, A. C. (1990). *Applied behavior analysis for teachers* (3rd ed.). Columbus, OH: Charles E. Merrill.

Cartwright, C. A., & Cartwright, G. P. (1974). *Developing observational skills* (2nd ed.). New York: McGraw-Hill.

Cullinan, D., Epstein, M. H., & Lloyd, J. W. (1983). *Behavior disorders of children and youth*. Englewood Cliffs, NJ: Prentice-Hall.

Evans, S. S., & Evans, W. H. (1987). Behavior change and the ecological model, *The Pointer*, 31 (3), 9–13.

Evans, S. S., Evans, W. H., & Mercer, C. D. (1986). *Assessment for instruction*. Boston: Allyn and Bacon.

Evans, W. H., Evans, S. S., & Schmid, R. E. (1989). *Behavior and instructional management: An ecological approach*. Boston: Allyn and Bacon.

Good, T. L., & Brophy, J. E. (1987). *Looking in classrooms*. New York: Harper and Row.

Long, N. J., Morse, W. C., & Newman, R. G. (1980). *Conflict in the classroom* (4th ed.). Belmont, CA: Wadsworth.

McLoughlin, J. A., & Lewis, R. B. (1990). *Assessing special students* (3rd ed.). Columbus, OH: Charles E. Merrill.

Sparzo, F. J., & Poteet, J. A. (1989). *Classroom behavior: Detecting and correcting special needs*. Boston: Allyn and Bacon.

Zentall, S. S. (1983). Learning environments: A review of physical and temporal factors, *Exceptional Education Quarterly*, 4 (2), 90–110.

Zigmond, N., Vallecorsa, A., & Silverman, R. (1983). *Assessment for instructional planning*. Englewood Cliffs, NJ: Prentice-Hall.

PART II

AN ECOLOGICAL APPROACH TO CORRECTING INSTRUCTIONAL MANAGEMENT PROBLEMS

Correcting instructional problems depends upon precise detection. Without exact identification, there can be no assurance that the intervention will focus upon an appropriate behavior or element of the environment. Moreover, this assessment process allows for examination of the ways that students, teachers, and educational environments change. This information allows the teacher to focus efforts on relevant behavioral and environmental variables.

What happens in the home and community has a dramatic impact upon the student's school behavior. Witness the child who brings to school values or methods of conflict resolution that are significantly different from those expected in the school setting or even the student who is not encouraged or does not have a sufficient place in the home to complete homework. On a larger scale, a community loses interest in and fails to support an educational program that appears irrelevant and uninvolved. Unfortunately, accusations and confrontation often result from these problems, and then everyone loses.

In much the same manner, the organization and implementation of the total school program has a dramatic impact upon the instructional program. Classrooms reside within schools and are thus affected by the rules, expectations, and functioning of the school as a whole. The effectiveness of a superlative instructional program within a classroom may, for example, be adversely affected by poor school leadership, an unfair discipline program, or a general attitude of failure within the school.

All of this illustrates that the correction of instructional problems must encompass a host of variables from within and outside of the actual classroom. When home, community, and school efforts are well organized and in harmony with the classroom instructional program, the potential for student learning is enhanced. Perhaps just as important though, parents and the community become involved. The school becomes something to fight for rather than with.

In Part II, a variety of methods is presented for use in the home, community, and school to support and extend the efforts of the classroom teacher. The focus is upon establishing a coherent partnership that aids students, teachers, and parents.

Chapter 4 provides guidelines for involving parents and community members in the educational program. Unfortunately, a wealth of resources and services present in a community often go unused. Harnessing even a small number of these resources and services could have great impact on an instructional program. Also detailed in Chapter 4 are a variety of methods that can be used to create a home-classroom alliance. Guidelines for homework and educational activities that may be used in the home are presented.

Chapter 5 illustrates the necessity of comprehensive, schoolwide educational planning. Correcting a student's instructional problems may be extraordinarily complex, requiring the efforts of more than just an individual teacher. It is thus essential that interventions encompass the total school program.

Proposed in these chapters is an educational partnership between home, community, and school: A partnership in which the efforts of one build upon the accomplishments and efforts of the other. This type of organization is difficult for all involved; however, the benefits are more than worth the effort.

CHAPTER 4
INTERVENING IN THE HOME AND COMMUNITY

DETECTION   Watch for these problems:

- Students are often tardy or absent.
- Students fail to complete homework.
- Students show signs of tiredness, excessive illness, hunger, and inadequate or inappropriate clothing.
- Parents or students justify breaking rules.
- Teachers receive reports of abuse or illegal activity.

Students' experiences at home and in the community have a dramatic effect on the behavior and values they bring to the classroom setting. Problems occur if these behaviors and values differ significantly from those expected in the school setting. Moreover, the best formulated instructional intervention has little chance of success if there is a significant problem or lack of resources in the home or community.

When a significant home or community problem affects school performance, the question is not one of whether to intervene but rather who should intervene initially and later on. Some interventions, such as providing instruction concerning homework or tutoring, may be easily addressed by the classroom teacher. Other more serious problems, however, require involvement of a wide array of professionals who have the time and expertise to comprehensively address the apparent problem. The classroom teacher does not have the expertise and cannot single-handedly solve all of the student's problems. To attempt to do so almost insures that a difficult situation will be made much worse.

CORRECTION   Try these strategies:

1. *Refer students to social service or community agencies.*

     Classroom problems may be due to a lack of basic resources, such as food, clothing, or housing, or result from an unstable family environment. Teachers who suspect these types of problems should discreetly make appropriate school authorities aware of their concerns. Even more discretion must be exercised when approaching parents about the need for social services. Embarrassment, guilt, blame, rejection of services, and ugly confrontations may ensue if parents are approached in an inappropriate manner.

●●

An Instructional Problem

Stephanie's homework and behavior in school had definitely made a change for the worse. Mr. Moore, Stephanie's seventh-grade home-room teacher, noted that while the change had been somewhat gradual, it had now reached crisis proportions. Stephanie always seemed to be tired and grouchy and constantly snapped at her teachers and peers; her homework, which was now rarely completed, was unbelievably messy.

     With the assistance of Ms. Whitlock, the school guidance counselor, a conference was held with Stephanie's mother. What could have been an emotionally charged situation was handled with care and consideration. It became apparent that Stephanie's family had an immediate need for a broad range of social services. Given this information, as well as a positive parent relationship, Ms. Whitlock was able to assist Stephanie's mother in contacting social agencies for needed services.

     Mr. Moore immediately noted a slight improvement in Stephanie's classroom behavior. While the problem had not yet been rectified, at least the conditions that could foster a permanent change had been addressed.

●●

a. *Form a team.* It is absolutely critical that the parent be approached as part of a team whose task is to provide the best possible learning environment for the child. Meetings with this team should be designed to identify the needs of the student and family, the agencies that can meet these needs, and the responsibilities of each member of the team in obtaining and using these services. If the team meetings are conducted in a compassionate manner and designed to seriously and fully include the parent and child, there is an increased probability that the services will be used and well coordinated. If not, the attempt to provide services, however well intended, may be viewed as just another example of unwanted intrusion by a public institution.

b. *Identify available resources.* Teachers must be aware of the array of social and health care services available in a community. Often, community mental health or informal referral centers provide booklets that detail private and public services available, as well as eligibility requirements. Information concerning services can also be obtained from parent support groups, churches and synagogues, youth groups, hospitals, and colleges and universities. Armed with this information, the teacher can be a knowledgeable member of the team.

●●●

An Instructional Problem

Now that he was president of Edgewood Elementary's PTA, Mr. Posnett decided that he would be in a position to make some needed improvements in the school. He could never remember a time in the four years that his children had attended the school that there had been adequate playground equipment, and frankly, even a cursory inspection of the school provided evidence that painting and landscaping were needed. It seemed that everyone recognized the need, but no one did anything about it. Mr. Posnett was enough of a realist to admit that completing needed repairs and providing playground equipment wouldn't solve all of the school's problems, but he also realized that these changes would improve the situation.

Mr. Posnett's first step was to form a committee, in conjunction with school authorities, to examine the need for repairs and equipment. After an agreement was reached, the committee hammered out a plan for landscaping, painting, and building playground equipment. Each member of the committee was asked to form a group of parents, teachers, and students, and obtain specific materials that could be used in the repairs. Once these materials were obtained, two weekend workdays were scheduled. Careful scheduling allowed members of the community, along with parents, students, and teachers, to contribute a reasonable amount of time to the project. As nothing like this had ever happened in the area, these workdays drew the attention of the media.

When the project was completed, the school was certainly more attractive. Even more important, however, a lot of people who had never really been involved in the life of the school now saw it and what went on there as critically important.

●●

2. *Obtain needed educational resources and services from the community.*

An incredible wealth of talent, resources, and personnel is present in communities, yet goes unused. The coordinated use of these services does much to enhance the educational program, not only by providing necessary services and resources to the school but also by linking the school to the community. As a result, the school becomes an integral part of the community and is more fully supported by parents and community leaders alike. There are a variety of ways in which the community can be encouraged to become involved in the school:

a. *Seek volunteers.* Classroom volunteers can be obtained from service agencies, colleges and universities, guilds, retirement centers, government, and private industry. Some volunteers can serve as tutors, while others can enhance instruction in academic areas such as science, social studies, and art by sharing past experiences or demonstrating skills.

b. *Collect information.* Businesses and agencies can provide information about training related to a wide variety of occupations. This information can be used in the instructional program or serve as motivation for students interested in specific occupations. Additionally, businesses and agencies can be used for fieldtrips and may serve as sources for summer and after-school employment.

c. *Request donations.* Donations of material, labor, money, and scholarships can be obtained from businesses, civic groups, and public and private agencies. In many cases, stores prefer (for tax reasons) to donate unsold inventory to schools or charitable agencies. Before soliciting these resources, school district procedures should be examined and the specific needs of the school assessed. This eliminates embarrassing problems at a later date and ensures that the resources obtained will be used.

Labor for using or applying donations can be obtained by working with civic groups or qualified parents of students. As with resources, the use of labor must be carefully coordinated so as to ensure that school procedures are adhered to and that labor is not wasted.

Community resources can be used to enhance virtually all elements of the educational program. Playground equipment; paint; lighting fixtures; structural, electrical, and plumbing repairs; landscaping; instructional materials; rugs; window shades; furniture; fans; and art and physical education materials are but a few of the elements that could be obtained or improved.

3. *Facilitate home-school cooperation.*

Assist parents in establishing a home environment that supports and enhances the educational program. A wide variety of home activities can achieve this purpose:
- daily discussions of school activities
- monitoring television time
- modeling by parents of academic tasks, such as reading
- providing a quiet place, a specific time, and support for homework
- obtaining and using a library card
- discussing current events and daily problems
- rewarding school achievement and participation

a. *Inform parents.* Parents should be encouraged and informed of daily opportunities in the home to teach and foster student skills. This often necessitates a parent education program that illustrates ways in which daily activities can be used to teach and enhance skills and concepts taught in school. To implement such a program, it may be desirable to sponsor a parent newsletter that details practices found to be successful. Additionally, a parent-teacher communication system should be established to inform parents of the skills being taught in the classroom. This same system should allow parents and teachers to freely exchange information concerning successful strategies, as well as tactics that should be avoided.

b. *Encourage development of routines.* A home educational program should also seek to establish a climate in which personal responsibility, initiative, and hard work are rewarded. It should not be assumed that these traits occur spontaneously. Rather, they must be encouraged and planned for by the use of household routines that clearly delineate and reward completion of individual responsibilities. It must be remembered, however, that the child's participation, rather than perfection of the task, is the goal of the program.

c. *Plan for the completion of homework.* Student achievement can be significantly enhanced by homework that encourages use of skills learned in the classroom. Certainly, homework must be of an appropriate level of difficulty, thoroughly explained, relevant, and evaluated in a timely fashion. Moreover, the parent as well as the student should be fully informed of the teacher's policies and expectations concerning completion, accuracy, and grading. Parents must also communicate concerns and problems encountered while the student was completing his or her homework. This interactive process will do a great deal to enhance the education program.

Specific suggestions to facilitate the completion of homework include:

- Designate a time and place in which homework is to be completed, such as immediately after an afternoon snack at the kitchen table. (Generally, it is best to require that homework be completed before playtime).
- Encourage the student to bring home all materials necessary for completion of homework. A daily checklist may facilitate this process.
- Check homework for accuracy and neatness.
- Offer encouragement and recognition for effort.

4. *Establish a home tutoring program.*

Home tutoring can greatly assist in the learning and use of academic tasks. On the other hand, tutoring sessions can become horrendous and frustrate parent and child alike. It is important to provide guidelines for parents. For example:

- Coordinate carefully with the classroom teacher.
- Use the same general instructional procedures used in the classroom.
- Deal with only one clearly defined skill.
- Hold short lessons, perhaps 15 minutes.
- Reward rather than punish efforts.

●●●

An Instructional Problem

Ms. Kelly thought that with a little bit of assistance from home, Jason, a third-grader, could do much better in reading. Jason was reading at the second-grade level and had a variety of minor yet obvious problems that inhibited his reading.

A conference with Jason's parents was held and agreement was reached on a plan. Jason's parents would help him obtain a library card and allow him twice a week to select a book that he would read aloud to his parents before bed every night. Guidelines were given to the parents about how to gently ask questions about what was read and how to encourage the reading. Additionally, Jason's parents agreed to provide 10 minutes of after-school tutoring every day to Jason. Again, guidelines were given, with Ms. Kelly agreeing to send home a daily note on Jason's accomplishments and the skill that should be practiced at home.

The program went through some modification and required a unique level of cooperation. But in the end, Jason's reading improved, and Ms. Kelly had gained invaluable allies in Jason's parents.

●●

5. *Facilitate frequent, positive, and personal home-school communication.*
Virtually everyone in the United States receives some sort of form letter on a daily basis. We have become so immune to this form of communication that regardless of the intent of the message, the letter is generally relegated to the garbage can, often unopened. Parent-school communication is similarly incomplete and irrelevant when schools adopt impersonal form letters as their primary means of communication with parents. Most important, perhaps, is the missed chance for establishing a close relationship between home and school.

While form letters notifying parents of school events and activities do have a place, there is a critical need for a comprehensive range of personal and direct methods of communication. Specifically:

a. *Conduct parent conferences in which there is a free and civil exchange of ideas and expectations.* Establish a clear goal, fastidiously avoid placing blame and using jargon, develop a climate of rapport, and identify mutually agreed upon strategies. Parents and teachers should have equal opportunities to address concerns.
b. *Issue frequent oral and written progress notes that detail the student's successes and the skills being addressed in the classroom, not failures and problems.*

Effective communication leads to effective strategies, but it also leads to an educational climate in which parents and teachers are working together on mutually agreed upon goals. In such a setting, education becomes an effective partnership.

CHAPTER 5
INTERVENING IN THE TOTAL SCHOOL SETTING

DETECTION

Watch for these problems:

- Excessive punishment is used in the school.
- The school lacks an organized curriculum across subject areas and grade levels.
- The school curricula lack relevance.
- There is little meaningful teacher and parent input for the development of the instructional program.
- Poor communication exists between parents, students, teachers, and administrators.
- Student failure and retention rates are high.
- The school leadership is ineffective.
- School staff have developed negative expectations.

The manner in which the classroom instructional program is implemented is constantly affected by the organization of the total school program. Schools that are effective generally foster classrooms that are effective. Likewise, it is extremely difficult for the individual teacher to implement an effective instructional program when the total school program is disorganized and incoherent.

Curricula, discipline, grading, materials, and even the skill levels of students in each classroom are but a few of the elements of the educational program not solely under the direct control of the teacher but rather are controlled at the school or district level. Therefore, instructional management must be comprehensive and account for the total school setting.

CORRECTION

Try these strategies:

1. *Develop a comprehensive discipline system.*

In far too many cases, discipline is always punitive and designed solely as a means of responding to and suppressing inappropriate behavior. In these cases, discipline becomes merely a reaction to student behavior and fails to prompt and promote appropriate responses. Moreover, chaos reigns when this type of discipline program is arbitrarily enforced in an entire school.

A schoolwide discipline program should:
- be fair and effective
- provide a range of interventions and rules for application
- have as its central goal prevention of inappropriate student behavior
- be seen as a means for assisting implementation of the instructional program, rather than an end in itself
- reflect beliefs of teachers, students, and parents

A more comprehensive discussion of specific classroom discipline systems is presented in Chapter 8.

●●●

An Instructional Problem

The instructional program at Woodbine Middle School was, to put it mildly, confusing. The principal, Mr. Redish, in a misguided attempt at educational reform, had decided to eliminate all of the hierarchies that detailed what skills were to be taught at each grade level. He also eliminated ringing bells to indicate beginnings and ends of classes because he believed this practice belittled the staff and students. Perhaps most confusing, however, to staff and students was that every six weeks, the order of classes changed, and two new "exploratory" classes began.

Few of the staff saw the need for the exploratory classes. But Mr. Redish believed that entirely too much time was consumed teaching academic subject areas. He initiated a program in which every six weeks, each staff member would teach two nonacademic courses that would appeal to the interests of the students.

In their evaluation of the school, the Program Review Team from the Department of Education found that the educational program at Woodbine was unfocused and misguided. By their calculations, approximately a third of every school day was spent in pursuit of so-called exploratory activities such as macrame. They found little organization to the curriculum; each teacher was the sole judge of what should be taught. And the situation with the bells resulted in nothing short of pandemonium. There was no coordination of when students were to be released from or expected in class. This resulted in a nearly constant flow of students and noise in the hall.

The review team did note that there were some outstanding teachers in the school, but they were totally demoralized by the lack of organization and their inability to provide input for program development. What had resulted, according to the review team, was a school with good teachers who were prevented from being good teachers.

●●

2. *Develop a relevant, multifaceted curriculum.*

Schools serve a broad range of students who have a wide variety of interests and varied levels of skill development. Additionally, some students have college as their goal, others wish to pursue a vocational program, and still others are in a more formative stage and have no specific purpose for their education. These diverse needs clearly point to why a school curriculum must allow numerous choices and match the unique needs of the student. Such a curriculum is formed along a variety of guidelines:

a. *Focus on an agreed upon series of goals and objectives.* A curriculum that is developed by a small, select group of administrators or consultants may not reflect the needs of the community or those who have to implement or consume the product. As a result, those excluded from the development may be less likely to actually implement or participate in the program. For this reason, parents, teachers, and even students should assist in identifying the goals of the curriculum. Moreover, this participation should not be illusory but a substantive and an integral part of the development, implementation, and adaptation of the curriculum.

b. *Offer a common core of courses.* The curriculum development process will lead to identification of a series of commonly held goals and skills that are essential to all students. These skills may then be taught in a core of courses required of all students, including reading, math, language arts, science, social studies, the arts, and physical education. Times and needs change, however; there should be periodic reexamination of the skills taught in the core curriculum.

c. *Include a diversity of educational experiences and activities.* An array of age-appropriate vocational education programs, college preparatory classes, and elective courses must be offered if schools are to meet the varied needs of students. Schools who do not offer comprehensive programs and have a "one-size-fits-all curriculum" fail in this regard. This leads to student apathy and contributes to school failure and drop-out.

The educational program must also offer diverse extracurricular activities. Participation in sports, music, and clubs allows students an opportunity to gain additional skills and knowledge, provides a forum for creativity, and fosters development of appropriate social and personal skills. Moreover, some students find school rewarding largely because of participation in extracurricular activities. Thus, eliminating them or precluding participation often inadvertently removes the reason many students attend school.

d. *Organize the presentation of the instructional program.* For the instructional program to be coherent, it must be presented in an organized manner. A hierarchy of skills must be developed for each academic area, detailing a sequence of skills taught in each area and grade level and thus providing continuity across grade levels. A curriculum hierarchy in math, for example, may indicate that basic addition facts (two-digit addition) should be taught in first grade and followed in second-grade by "carrying."

A curriculum hierarchy should never be used, however, to artificially inhibit student growth. Students who are reading and comprehending significantly above grade level should not be forced to endure a reading program that is appropriate for the grade but far too easy for their level of development. To do so ensures boredom.

It is also critical that the instructional program within the school be well organized. Rules and expectations should be clearly stated and a fair routine established for students and teachers alike.

3. *Offer an array of services and settings.*

Services and settings should be just as varied as the curriculum. Some students, for example, are best served in a setting with little formal structure and in which the teacher serves more as a facilitator than a director of activities. But other students may need a broad array of supportive educational and social services, and may be best served in a highly structured classroom in which there is a low student-teacher ratio. Schools should have a range of settings, from least to most restrictive. While the regular classroom is the least restrictive, some students might be better served in more restrictive settings, such as part-time special classes, full-time special classes, special schools, or mental health facilities.

Certainly, placement in a more restrictive setting should be cautiously considered. Movement to a more restrictive setting must be based upon the real educational needs of the student and not the convenience of the school staff. The stigma attached to a more restrictive placement can be significant and cause teachers and peers to perceive and interact with the student in a negative and unwarranted manner.

4. *Frequently evaluate student progress.*

Students who experience success in school are more likely to enjoy and profit from the instructional program. Frequent assessment allows numerous opportunities for students to experience success. Additionally, frequent assessment alerts teachers to instructional problems so that interventions can be made in a timely manner.

Students must also believe that success is attainable. Those who have a long history of failure in school and believe that there is little chance for success may simply give up. The challenge for the school is to institute evaluation procedures that encourage and allow students frequent opportunities to meet achievable goals on relevant tasks.

5. *Plan for effective and coordinated leadership.*

Effective schools are well-managed places in which the instructional program is organized to meet the unique needs of each learner. Certainly, these schools provide a broad array of relevant educational and extracurricular experiences and have a carefully coordinated discipline program. They also share another, perhaps more critical component—leadership.

Effective educational leadership takes many forms, but in most cases, successful leaders are those who encourage prudent experimentation; provide resources and organization to the entire instructional program so that collective goals of the school can be met; build morale among teachers, staff, and students; and share responsibility for the development and implementation of the educational program. Adversarial relationships between administrators and teachers are uncommon in these schools, and support is equally provided to all staff. The opinions of staff, students, and teachers are valued; there are ample opportunities for relevant professional development; and recognition is quickly and freely provided for all efforts and achievements.

In effective schools, leaders establish a climate in which all resources are directed at providing a relevant, safe, effective, and satisfying instructional environment. As a result, the curriculum is not merely an extension of the status quo. Rather, it is constantly developing through the input of students, teachers, and parents.

●●●

An Instructional Problem

Jessie, a fifth-grader, had just transferred to Mayfield Elementary from a school in another state. In reviewing his cumulative folder, Mr. Ramon, Jessie's fifth-grade teacher, noted a history of mild behavior and academic problems and poor grades. He also noted numerous comments by prior teachers about Jessie's bad attitude and lack of attention in class.

While these comments were disturbing to Mr. Ramon, he had witnessed few of these problems in the 12 weeks since Jessie had enrolled at Mayfield. Initially, Jessie had been somewhat sullen, but after a very positive parent conference and several sessions with the school counselor, Jessie's behavior and attitude improved dramatically.

What Mr. Ramon now saw was a student who was eager to learn and took great pride in having his artwork and math papers displayed on the bulletin board. Most of all, Jessie loved displaying his daily progress chart in reading and math and lived for the award certificates and the accompanying candy from the principal.

Mr. Ramon questioned Jessie about the puzzling dichotomy between past and present performance. Jessie responded simply, "At the other school, no one every paid any attention to me unless I did something wrong. Here it's different. The work is more interesting, and you expect and help me to learn. It's kind of like we're on the same team."

● ●

6. *Communicate positive expectations.*

Successful schools are those that expect and encourage student growth; seek participation by the community, parents, and students; and provide teachers an active role in the development and implementation of the instructional program. Teachers and administrators in these schools have a commitment to increased student learning and do not establish expectations that artificially limit student growth.

A great deal of professional literature has clearly demonstrated that teacher behavior is affected by negative expectations. In short, teachers provide less effective assistance and more negative feedback if they believe that students are incapable or unwilling to learn. These students, as a result, fail to master necessary academic material and simultaneously develop negative attitudes about learning and school. This cyclical pattern produces frustration for both students and teachers.

Contrast this, however, to schools that establish a climate in which individuality is encouraged and services and efforts are carefully coordinated. In these schools, teachers and administrators share professionalism that encourages active participation. Instructional problems are not viewed as simply validations of negative expectations but rather as opportunities for learning. Encouragement, effort, and shared responsibility are the hallmarks of these schools. In short, these schools foster positive expectations and establish a climate in which learning will occur and satisfaction will result.

REFLECTIONS

1. The organization of Part II reflects that special needs are not just student specific; instead, they are an outcome of complex student-environment interactions. List five ways you might intervene and positively influence a student's ecosystem.
2. List and consider the roles and responsibilities of persons you might engage in carrying out a home-community intervention.
3. Many of the difficulties students have are the product of either an ineffective discipline system or a classroom curriculum that is ill suited to individual abilities and interests. Describe the important steps you could take to remedy a flawed discipline system and an inadequate curriculum.
4. Reread Chapter 4 and develop guidelines that could assist parents in facilitating homework and enhancing the content taught in the classroom.
5. After rereading Chapter 5, list at least 10 critical factors each for elementary, middle, and high school that must be addressed in the development and implementation of an effective educational program. Compare and contrast the differences among the three levels of schooling.
6. Interview students to determine how specific school-based extracurricular activities affect their performance in the educational program. Ask how they would improve extracurricular activities in their school.
7. Interview school and social service personnel, and compile a list of services available in your community. Describe how individuals qualify for these programs and the difficulties encountered in obtaining services.
8. Interview teachers and parents of elementary, middle, and high school students, and compile a list of at least five impediments to home-school interaction and five ways that this relationship could be enhanced. Compare and contrast the differing perceptions of parents and teachers.
9. Observe and interview a teacher and an administrator from a local elementary, middle, or high school, and develop a list of 10 school practices that hinder and enhance development and implementation of an effective educational program.
10. In addition to the information presented in Chapters 4 and 5, consult other textbooks that focus on ways to establish and maintain a classroom climate that is consonant with quality teaching and learning. Compare information in these chapters with that from the following sources:

    Cegelka, P. A. (1981). Career education. In A. E. Blackhurst & W. H. Berdine (Eds.), *An introduction to special education*. Boston: Little, Brown.
    Jones, V. F., & Jones, L. S. (1990). *Comprehensive classroom management* (3rd ed.). Boston: Allyn and Bacon.
    Mendler, A. N., & Curwin, R. L. (1983). *Taking charge in the classroom*. Reston, VA.: Reston.

Paine, S. C., Radicchi, J., Rosellini, L. C., Deutschman, L., & Darsch, C. B. (1983). *Structuring your classroom for academic success*. Champaign, IL: Research Press.

Shea, T. M., & Bauer, A. M. (1987). *Teaching children and youth with behavior disorders* (2nd ed.). Englewood Cliffs, NJ: Prentice-Hall.

U.S. Department of Education. (1986). *What works: Research about teaching and learning*. Washington, DC: Author.

PART III

DETECTION AND CORRECTION AT WORK IN THE CLASSROOM

As illustrated in Part II, parents and members of the community play a vital role in the correction of instructional problems. As allies, they help forge a permanent educational bond that benefits students, parents, and teachers.

Also critical in this process are the conditions in the school, or the educational climate. Effective classroom instructional programs will be supported in schools that have high expectations, well-coordinated programs, and a highly motivated staff. This clearly points to the necessity of comprehensive ecological planning, including careful consideration of how all elements of various environments fit together and support each other.

In Part III, a broad array of tactics is presented for classroom use in the correction of instructional problems. While some factors such as room size and spacing of windows may hinder an educational program, it is in the classroom that the teacher has the most control over environmental events. Discipline plans, room organization, time management, instructional grouping, materials, and instructional procedures are all under the the direct control of the classroom teacher and may be modified in order to accommodate the instructional needs of students.

Chapter 6 details the importance of preventive instructional planning. A great deal of misbehavior can be eliminated and learning increased by careful planning. Many of these same principles carry over into Chapter 7, which discusses in depth the conditions necessary for producing an effective learning environment. These chapters emphasize the importance of establishing a climate in which learning is encouraged and instructional procedures are focused upon meeting students' individual needs.

Discipline plans are examined in Chapter 8, with emphasis on development of appropriate social behaviors and use and enforcement of classroom rules. It is difficult for learning to occur in settings in which there is an unacceptable level of misbehavior and the teacher's time is spent resolving behavior problems, rather than teaching. A variety of resolution techniques is presented in this chapter.

Room layout and organization are presented in Chapter 9 and scheduling and time management in Chapter 10. Attention is given to establishing a room plan and routine that are efficient, effective, and accommodate the needs of the teacher, as well as the students. If room organization and time management are not carefully addressed, the instructional program can become extremely and unnecessarily disorganized, thus causing students and teachers to waste valuable time and energy.

The use of a variety of instructional groupings is examined in Chapter 11. It is simply impossible in a classroom setting, to instruct each student individually on a constant basis. For this and a variety of others reasons, instructional groupings are necessary and desirable.

The materials that students use must be carefully selected and adapted to meet their individual needs. Chapter 12 provides guidelines for development and appropriate use of instructional materials.

A variety of instructional procedures is examined in Chapter 13. Special attention is given to matching instructional methods to the student's stage of learning. These procedures, as well as positive grading tactics, create an environment that fosters student success.

Even the best of teachers will become frustrated and encounter difficulties in dealing with parents, students, and professional peers. The final chapter, 14, examines ways of preventing teacher burnout and methods for resolving the inevitable conflicts that occur in teaching.

The material presented in Part III is designed to assist the teacher in establishing a classroom that is efficient and effective. In addition, this information should make teaching and learning fun and rewarding, which is an equally important goal.

CHAPTER 6
PREVENTIVE INSTRUCTIONAL PLANNING

DETECTION

Watch for these problems:

- Teachers have low expectations of academic performance from students.
- The instructional program is confusing or poorly organized.
- Inadequate time is allotted for classroom instruction.
- Teachers offer little or no performance feedback to students.
- The classroom situation is one in which praise is ineffective.

Preventive planning can eliminate a significant number of instructional and behavior management problems. Classrooms in which preventive planning is not practiced are chaotic and force the teacher into a reactive role. This in turn creates a climate in which learning becomes merely a matter of chance and teacher dissatisfaction is almost certain.

Preventive planning necessitates careful coordination of all elements of the instructional program. This chapter illustrates how these diverse elements can be organized to create an effective instructional environment and provides a framework for use of the more detailed information provided in remaining chapters.

•••

An Instructional Problem

In her first year of teaching, Kelly Spesman was careful to listen to more experienced teachers in order to pick up ideas for solving classroom problems. At lunch, the third-grade team was discussing several children. "Some kids are just slow," said Anne. "That's right," chimed in Martha. "Kids like Demetrious are never going to be able to do what the rest of the kids can do." "I don't expect too much," added Lou. "If they just behave, that's good enough." That afternoon, Kelly informed the four children in her lowest-achieving group that the workbook was very hard and instructed them, "Just do what you can, and don't worry about the rest."

•••

CORRECTION

Try these strategies:

1. *Set and hold high expectations for student performance.*

When teachers hold and communicate high expectations for student learning, achievement is increased. When teachers indicate that less is expected of one group of children than others in the class, it is likely that that group will achieve less. Even the kindest delivered, best intentioned statement of compromise—"Oh Patrick, your group can't do that exercise. Why don't you do a drill sheet until the rest of the class has finished?"—relays expectations about Patrick and his group's ability to function in the classroom.

Teachers sometimes attribute the success of achieving students to their teaching ability and inadequate achievement to the students' lack of ability, weak motivation, or poor home environment. This transfer of responsibility for poor achievement from teacher to student results in teachers ignoring the classroom structures and procedures demonstrated to improve academic success. As a group, however, effective teachers believe that all students can learn and take firm responsibility for academic performance at all levels of achievement.

Numerous factors contribute to how a teacher perceives a student's potential. Many of the often cited factors (number of low-achieving students in a classroom, teacher bias, and teacher training, for example) are supported by little or no reliable evidence. School climate and administrative support, on the other hand, clearly control how a teacher perceives low-achieving students. In schools where the faculty believe children can learn and take personal responsibility for the performance of each child, perceptions and values of individual teachers tend to reflect those of the entire group. Likewise, a school administration that insists teachers take responsibility for the achievement of each student and acts to support teachers influences how low achievers are perceived. Professional peer pressure also directly influences how individual teachers view low-achieving children. Listening to derogatory comments— such as "You are wasting your time with that kid; he will never learn," "What can you expect from a family like that?" or "She rides bus number 42, and all of those kids are low"—is bound to affect a teacher's expectations for achievement. Student beliefs about themselves also control to some degree teacher expectations. Children who acknowledge they are dumb, refuse to attempt the work, and are disruptive affect teacher expectations.

Specific suggestions for demonstrating high expectations of students include:

a. *Give low achievers the same number of chances to perform as are given to high achievers.* During class discussion, for example, make a point of alternating between calling on a high achiever and a low achiever. This increases the opportunity for low achievers to receive corrective feedback.

b. *When calling on a student, give the low achiever ample time to respond.* Count to 10, if necessary, to give the student time to formulate an answer. Follow the response with sufficient correction to get the student back on track, if need be. Give as much corrective feedback to low achievers as to high achievers.

c. *Do not praise low achievers for marginal or inadequate performance more often than high achievers.* There are times, of course, when classroom conditions dictate praising a marginal performance. The teacher, however, must be careful not to develop one standard for low-achieving students and another for high-achieving students. Also avoid being more critical of failure in the low achiever than in the high achiever.

d. *Prompt low achievers toward the correct response.* If an incorrect response is given, do not hesitate to take more time to offer cues and hints until the student can approximate an appropriate response. Guiding a student to an appropriate and acceptable answer is a technique used by all effective teachers.

e. *With low achievers, do not substitute seatwork and drill for interactive teaching.* Children who are permitted to practice errors or become frustrated because they don't know how to do a task are not very likely to become high achievers. Independent work should be used after interactive teaching has established understanding and a grasp of the skill to be learned.

f. *Tolerate fewer interruptions when working with low achievers than when working with high achievers.* Low achievers are often apt to avoid learning tasks by chatting, sharpening pencils, or asking irrelevant questions. These kinds of disruptions reduce the engaged time of the students who can least afford it.

g. *Be as enthusiastic with low achievers as with high achievers.* Enthusiasm stimulates attention and task engagement. Give the same smiles, eye contact, and responsiveness to low achievers as to high achievers.

●●●

An Instructional Problem

Mr. Delp said to Ms. James, "I am so excited about starting the unit on forest ecologies today. The kids are going to do an oral report, take a fieldtrip to the woods, and write a research paper."

"Oh," said Ms. James, "that sounds like a great unit. What are the kids going to learn?"

"I told you," replied Mr. Delp. "They are going to give oral reports and write papers. You know, that kind of stuff."

"C'mon Bill," said Ms. James. "What are your learning objectives for the kids?"

"I never bother with that," answered Mr. Delp. "If you have kids give reports and write papers, they always learn what they are supposed to."

●●●

2. *Implement effective instructional strategies.*

There are many strategies for providing classroom instruction. Sometimes a group of tactics is clustered and given a name, such as *mastery learning, individualized education, adaptive learning,* or *cognitive education.* To be effective in the classroom, a teacher must use an instructional strategy that includes the following elements: (a) clearly defined objectives, (b) a standard for minimum acceptable achievement, (c) a method for evaluating progress, and (d) remediation for students who do not meet the minimum achievement standard.

Attempting to teach without an instructional strategy results in teacher ineffectiveness. While there is no one best instructional system, there must be a system around which the teacher organizes learning activities for the classroom. The alternative is all negative—disorganization, disruptive behavior, teacher stress, and low achievement.

A number of factors control the selection and use of an instructional strategy by teachers. First, teacher-training programs must introduce individuals to the rationale for instructional strategies and provide opportunities for practice using various strategies. Second, school administrators must insist that teachers use instructional strategies in their teaching. Third, teachers must use peer pressure to ensure consistent use of instructional strategies by each faculty member. While no individual teacher should be forced to use a strategy he or she dislikes (for example, mastery learning or cognitive education), there should be a clear expectation that every teacher uses some strategy to enhance his or her organization for instruction.

Specific suggestions for effective instructional organization include:

a. *Carefully review the teacher's edition of the text to identify suggested objectives for the teaching unit.* Revise the objectives to fit the needs of the specific students to be taught. Discard the objectives that are not relevant and add new ones that are. Make certain each objective states (1) who is to achieve it, (2) the observable behavior the student will demonstrate, (3) under what conditions, and (4) how achievement will be measured.

b. *Establish a minimum standard of achievement for each objective aimed at each student.* This does not necessarily mean that each student will automatically achieve the standard; remediation may be necessary for some.

c. *Clearly communicate the standards to each student in the group and how he or she may achieve them.* There is a positive relationship between knowing what is expected and achieving it.

d. *Develop a method for sampling student progress along the way.* Several techniques may be used. Daily teacher questioning, for example, is an informal method of keeping track of both group and individual learning. Frequent quizzes over content will give a sample of each individual student's progress. Projects, presentations, and papers are all methods of evaluating the quantity and quality of student learning.

e. *Identify and provide enrichment and extension strategies for the unit objectives for those students who reach mastery earliest.*

f. *Provide regular remediation opportunities that are both teacher directed and peer assisted.* In planning peer-assisted remediation, keep in mind that (1) when high-achieving students work with low-achieving students, achievement benefits accrue primarily to the low achievers; (2) when high-achieving classmates work with high and low achievers, achievement benefits accrue to both groups; and (3) when low achievers work together without high achievers to provide assistance, achievement suffers.

g. *Develop a test that measures final mastery of the unit objectives for use in grading students, as well as for planning subsequent instruction.* Mastery tests may be given after each unit or after several units, perhaps to conform to the school marking periods.

●●

An Instructional Problem

The last daily announcement over the intercom was, "Grade reports are due in the office this Friday at 9:00 A.M." Bert Jerrinigan swallowed hard.He had not taught science to his third-graders for at least four weeks, and he was expected to report a six-week grade in two days.

Mr. Jerrinigan is an excellent teacher. Parents begin requesting him before their children have even finished the first-grade year. His problem, however, is that he has trouble ending a learning activity on time. In this marking term, for example, the class was so excited about working on their social studies projects that they consistently ran over into the time scheduled for science instruction.

●●

3. *Manage allocated learning time.*

Allocated learning time is the amount of time available for students to work on academic tasks during the school day. Time is the single most important commodity directly controlled by the teacher. There is little real difference between schools in time designated for the instructional day. While most schools schedule five or six hours for daily instructional activity, the critical factor is how that time is used. Increasing the time devoted to academic instruction within the school day increases student achievement. Consequently, a concerted effort to use the maximum available allocated learning time for academic instruction should be a high priority for teachers.

Actual allocated learning time is less than the total time scheduled for the instructional day. In the elementary school, art, music, and physical education instruction are regularly scheduled during the school week; assemblies and special events are common in the secondary school. Some students in a class may be scheduled for special support services, such as time in an exceptional education classroom. Activities such as these all deduct time from the instructional day and are not controlled by the classroom teacher. In reality, teachers have control only of the time that students are physically in their classrooms, and even that cannot all be devoted to instruction. The routine daily announcements and record management activities that begin most school days, for example, must be deducted from the time available for instruction.

Specific suggestions for managing allocated learning time include:

a. *Structure space.* Effective teachers arrange furnishings to accommodate the types of group activities they plan to use and to minimize disruptive movement of students around the classroom. If a teacher plans to use large-group presentations and smaller discussion groups for academic instruction, the arrangement of desks and tables should permit efficient transition between the two methods. The furnishings should also be arranged so a definite traffic pattern in and out of the work area(s) is established. An arrangement, for example, that creates a bottleneck in student movement at the room entrance will cause disruptions and loss of instructional time. Likewise, storage for materials, equipment, and student belongings that allows quick and easy access decreases delays and disruptions.

b. *Plan instruction.* Effective teachers seldom "wing it." They plan for every moment of instructional time and can succinctly state the objective of the activity in which the class is engaged. Both long- and short-term planning are used. For each grading period a teacher should know about and forecast time lost due to school vacations, scheduled assemblies, and other events requiring classroom activity. At the beginning of each school week, a teacher should prepare a written plan for daily activity that accounts for every available minute of allocated instructional time.

c. *Establish routines.* A teacher must plan for three kinds of activities within the instructional day: (1) academic (e.g., reading and math), (2) nonacademic (e.g., sharing and social relations), and (3) noninstructional (e.g., transitions, disruptions, and housekeeping). To the greatest extent possible, routines should increase the time given academic activities. Some suggestions for accomplishing this include:

1) Start and stop each element of the routine on time. Posting a schedule with the times for each daily activity may be sufficient for many classrooms. In other cases, an inexpensive timer with an alarm can be used to cue the beginning and/or end of an activity. Appointing a student as timekeeper to signal activity beginning and/or ending is also effective.

2) Reduce the transition time between classroom activities. Clearly announcing the end of one activity and the time allotted to prepare for the next is effective. In a voice that can be clearly heard, say, "Reading has ended. You have two minutes to put your reading materials away. Take out your math books and then look at me for directions." Rewarding those who are ready for the next activity will encourage those who are not to become more efficient.

3) Discourage interruptions by others (including staff and students) during instructional time. Inform the office staff that unless an emergency exists, the class is not to be interrupted with messages via the intercom. When a student is to leave school early, send him or her to the office at a specific time, rather than be interrupted with the message that the parents have arrived. Parents who arrive during instruction time and request a conference should be firmly referred to the office to make a conference appointment or wait until the teacher has a free period. Implement class traditions that discourage student or staff drop-in visits. Requiring, for example, that any person entering the room after instruction has begun must sing the day's lunchroom menu to the class will immediately eliminate most routine drop-in traffic.

d. *Communicate routines.* Students can follow a routine only if they know what it is. They should be informed of the daily routine and any changes in established procedures. Post the basic daily schedule in a location and of a size that is easily read in the classroom. A smaller schedule, including teacher free time, should be posted outside the classroom door.

e. *Reduce noninstructional activity.* Making announcements, taking roll, and collecting monies are part of the instructional day. Many noninstructional activities, however, can be eliminated or at least reduced in frequency. There are numerous methods for doing this. Start an instructional activity and do clerical tasks while the students are working. Get a student, aide, or volunteer to do these tasks. Work clerical and housekeeping tasks into the daily routine so that they are done unobtrusively as part of an instructional task. Completing an equipment inventory form, for example, can be turned into a math exercise for a group of students (How many items at a set cost are on the inventory? How many are missing? What is the difference?). Delay noninstructional tasks to be completed during a preparation period or time when academic instruction is not taking place.

f. *Manage the transition of students between rooms and teachers.* Student movement between locations can be made more efficient in a number of ways. The simplest is for teachers to step outside their classroom doors and supervise the students. Providing a simple activity that has a time limit and reward will decrease transition time. For example, putting a simple math problem, brain teaser, or pertinent trivia question on the board and providing a few extra-credit points to each student who, within two minutes of the bell, turns in the correct answer guarantees that most students will be in the room on time and working. For young children, direct instruction and practice in making a transition is necessary. For older students, a time card that notes departure and arrival time can be effective.

●●

An Instructional Problem

For some reason, Ms. Conroy's eighth-grade language arts students rarely complete an entire independent work assignment. Ella Conroy carefully plans academic work and has very appropriate objectives for each unit she presents to her students. She gives excellent directions for completing work, especially independent work, and checks to make certain every student understands what is expected. During the time students are working on assignments, Ella corrects papers and completes her daily reports and paperwork. She permits the students to talk with each other quietly and to move about the room, as long as it does not disturb anyone. In spite of her careful planning, the students just don't complete the amount of work that she expects of them.

●●

4. *Effectively motivate engaged time.*

Engaged time is the proportion of allocated learning time during which the student is paying attention and on-task. It is when the student appears to be actively engaged in the process of learning.

A teacher can be effective in squeezing every possible moment of allocated learning time from the instructional day and still find little actual learning by students. Learning requires presentation of academic instruction and active participation of the student in the process. Student participation is indicated by numerous behaviors, such as watching and listening to the teacher, asking relevant questions, making appropriate comments, and successfully completing exercises. If these indicators of student participation are absent or replaced by other behaviors, active engagement has been lost, and learning is unlikely to result.

Motivating students during engaged time depends on a number of factors, some of which are not controlled by the teacher. A student who is fatigued will be less engaged in instruction than one who is rested. Students who are hungry or anxious will also be difficult to motivate. On the other hand, teachers do control many important factors related to motivation. Selecting tasks to be completed, offering rewards and feedback, pacing, grouping, and advance organizers, for example, are all controlling factors that can be directly influenced by the teacher.

Specific suggestions for motivating students during engaged time include:

a. *Select learning tasks appropriate to the group.* Selecting learning tasks for the day does not depend on student interests or immediate teacher concerns but on the content to be learned. Two factors should guide the selection of academic classroom tasks. First, what are the most appropriate tasks for motivating students in engaged time? Some content will require the teacher to give a concise oral explanation or demonstration. Other content will require straightforward student practice of a skill or independent reading for fact acquisition. Second, are the tasks appropriate to the existing skill level of the students? Requiring students who have mastered basic addition facts to complete a large set of addition problems reduces engaged time, even though a majority of the students will complete some or all of the assignment. Asking a class of students with weak reading skills to independently read a selection of their textbook and complete a study guide will generate less engaged time than having the teacher outline the highpoints and identify important portions of the text prior to the students beginning the assignment.

b. *Use advance organizers.* Advance organizers provide structure for the learning tasks that follow and have been demonstrated to facilitate engaged time. An advance organizer (1) is a short set of verbal or visual information, (2) is presented prior to a learning task, and (3) demonstrates logical relationships in the learning task.

c. *Pace student work rate.* Effective teachers move through learning tasks at the most brisk rate a group can tolerate and still experience success. Groups who differ in achievement level will require different pacing rates. For instance, high-achieving groups will work at a faster pace than low-achieving groups. A teacher must, however, be alert to changes in the pacing rate required of a group due to academic progress. The pacing rate of a group that was initially low achieving but improves over time will need adjustment. Maximum engaged time and learning results from a balance between pacing and a high success rate.

d. *Monitor student reaction and provide feedback.* Effective teachers continuously watch the group for signs of confusion or inattention and refocus student engagement with feedback. Restating a student question to make it precise will assist the group to understand a concept. Providing ample wait time for a student to formulate a response draws all the students into the discussion. Simply informing a student to get back on the subject reengages the group in the learning task.

e. *Practice teacher "cruising."* Circulate among the members of the group to check on progress, prompt, and reinforce engaged time. Avoid sitting at a desk. Limit time spent with individual students to a few seconds at a time. Get the student working and then return with additional help and encouragement. Students who are completely off-task or unable to do the work should be given alternative tasks they can complete until remediation can be scheduled. Tell your group that you intend to make "desk calls." Every student working on-task with a specified amount of accuracy when you make your call will receive extra-credit points.

f. *Vary grouping for instruction.* Initially work with the entire group, then use small-group and individual instruction as needs emerge for enrichment, extension, or remediation. Maintain direct teacher involvement and provide teacher-student interaction throughout the entire lesson. These interactions should consist of questioning, answering, reacting, and explaining. Expect everyone to respond and participate.

g. *Praise students.* Praise should be contingent upon being actively engaged in the learning tasks. The teacher must state specifically what the student is doing when he or she receives the praise. Words and phrases such as "good," "good job," "O.K.," and "nice work" have little real effect on student behavior. It is more effective to say, "You have completed three of the questions correctly and are working on the fourth. That is excellent performance, and I appreciate it." Praise must also be sincere and varied according to the situation and to the preferences of the student being praised.

h. *Make assignments challenging but not impossible.* The ability to complete an assignment successfully motivates students to continue engaged time. Assignments that are too difficult for the group are frustrating and reduce engaged time.

i. *Make students accountable for their work.* Tell them exactly what is expected and when. Discuss evaluation standards and any alternatives that will be accepted. Specify the consequences for not completing assignments and follow through.

●●

An Instructional Problem

Sara Holland is confused. Her professors and colleagues all indicated that praise increased the amount of work a student would produce. She is careful to praise her students frequently. For example, she has a habit of saying "good work," "way to go," or "I like it" whenever a student is on-task or has performed appropriately. For the past two weeks, Sara has been especially conscientious about praising Ivey Thomas in order to increase her engaged time. It hasn't worked. In fact, the amount of time Ivey is engaged in assigned academic work has decreased.

●●

5. *Use praise effectively.*

It is well documented that reinforcement techniques can be used to reduce disruptive student behaviors and increase positive behaviors—those that have a direct relationship with academic achievement. Praise is a positive teacher response that goes beyond corrective feedback ("That's the correct answer.") to provide students a status statement ("Your answer was thorough and well thought out.").

To be effective, teacher praise must be reinforcing to the student. That is, it must be contingent upon performance of a specific behavior, identify the behavior being reinforced, and be sincere and convincing. Unfortunately, praise is much misused by teachers. Teacher praise is often a reaction elicited and reinforced by students themselves. Moreover, much praise intended to be reinforcing is not because it is noncontingent, nonspecific, and uncredible. And when praise is intended to control disruptive behavior, it is directed at the students least concerned with pleasing the teacher.

In a learning situation the teacher seeks to praise an appropriate student response, believing that a positive relationship exists between praise and achievement. Responses, however, must be elicited. The thing that elicits a response is called a *stimulus*. A question asked in class, an exercise in a textbook, a word on a spelling test, a division problem, or a command to action are all stimuli used to provide the student with information needed to make a correct response. The response is the answer given in relation to the stimulus presented. For praise, the controlling factors are stimuli clear and unambiguous enough for students to produce a response and a judgement whether the response is acceptable or unacceptable. Thus, students must discriminate among possible responses, and teachers must determine correctness of the response elicited before praise can be given or withheld.

Specific suggestions for using praise effectively include:

a. *Provide clear stimuli.* Students must be able to understand and discriminate what is being asked of them in order to respond. Generally, teachers ask two types of questions. One calls for a short, factual answer that the student does or doesn't know. Questions of this type should be briskly paced but followed by ample wait time for a response. In presenting this kind of stimulus ask only one question at a time. For instance, asking the name of the main character in the story and where he was going is a double question. Double questions often produce responses that confuse both the teacher and student. A second type of stimuli requires reasoning from the student. These questions require both facts and a consideration of how and why relationships exist. Stimulus clarity is critical both for the student to respond and the teacher to evaluate the response. Asking "Why did Stinkey Charlie become angry?" requires the student to consider anger and what events in the story may have triggered it in Charlie. The response can be evaluated against the context of the story. For these kinds of stimuli pacing is slower and more deliberate.

b. *Praise contingently.* Teacher praise should immediately follow performance of a desired behavior. List the general behaviors for which all students will be praised (correct response to a direct question, completion of an assignment, quiet work) and for which individuals will be praised (Angela for spontaneous participation, Danny for readable handwriting). Establish the habit of praising only when a response is accurate and appropriate. Patrick, for example, should not be praised for shouting out a correct response if Cory was called on.

c. *Praise specifically.* It is critical to state the particulars of the response in the praise statement. Replying "good work" when Johnnie responds "24" to the question "How much is 3 times 8?" is not praise. It only provides feedback that Johnnie gave the correct answer. Praise would be to reply, "That is a hard one to remember, and you had to think about it to get it right. Good work." To praise, one must state specifically what part of the response was critical.

d. *Praise sincerely.* Praise, to be effective, must focus on a response that is praiseworthy and delivered honestly. Students are quick to see that praise given indiscriminately and as small talk is valueless and thus discount future praise accordingly. Likewise, students will reject praise statements accompanied by negative nonverbal gestures or facial expressions. Using praise carries the responsibility of clearly meaning the words spoken to be an honest reward for a worthwhile response.

e. *Adjust the frequency of praise.* Teachers have a fixed amount of time they can give to a class of students; therefore, they cannot be expected to praise every response elicited. Consequently, praise should be most frequent when students are learning a new skill or beginning an unfamiliar task. When an academic skill or social behavior is to be maintained over time, praise should be intermittent.

●●●

An Instructional Problem

Students in the senior English honors class have struggled all year with mastering the content. At the beginning of each new unit there is a period of a few days or a week when few of the students don't complain about how hard the class is. Ms. DeAnglis, the teacher, begins each unit by distributing a unit outline, a list of the required readings, and a set of introductory exercises. Only when the introductory exercises are completed does Ms. DeAnglis begin to discuss the topic content with the students.

●●●

6. *Implement interactive teaching practices.*

Effective instruction is based on teaching a common set of skill objectives to the whole class and expecting that all students will attain or exceed a performance standard. Some students will need extra time and corrective instruction, and others will need enrichment activity. This interactive help is given in practice, feedback, and reinstruction. The teacher must direct these practices, structure and pace the learning, ensure continuity, and maintain maximum engaged time. Interactive teaching has built-in mastery indicators. The teacher obtains feedback to identify the students who need additional time and instruction. Equally important, interactions signal when practice is excessive and the class should move on to new tasks.

A basic conceptual sequence appears to underlie interactive teaching. First, student attention is directed to the material to be learned through cues such as a call for attention and advance organizers. Next, students become actively engaged with the content of the material. Feedback directs the teacher to proceed or provide alternative explanations and demonstrations of what is to be mastered. Third, students are rewarded for their efforts at learning with praise, directing attention to the desired responses. Finally, interactive practice with the instructor and corrective feedback show students which areas need more work and require independent practice. The interactive sequence as a whole is more important than any one of its components.

Numerous factors affect the interactive teaching process. Learning objectives and materials available for instruction, control how a teacher approaches a group of students. Size of class controls how much time a teacher can give an individual student. Likewise, the academic and behavioral level of the group dictates application of materials, direction of interactions, and selection of learning activities. Other important factors are the time of day the group receives instruction and the time of year instruction is begun. Thus, a complex learning unit, requiring a high degree of concentration and effort from the students, might be better scheduled at a time other than late in the afternoon following physical education. Likewise, rather than begin a new unit the week prior to Christmas vacation, it would be better to begin after the holiday so teaching would be uninterrupted.

Specific suggestions for implementing interactive teaching practices include:

a. *Establish a performance standard for the learning unit.* If the specific group must master 7 of 10 learning objectives in order to move to the next instructional unit, the mastery performance standard is set at 70%. The teacher anticipates that every student will reach or exceed the standard of 70%. Grades must be pegged to various levels of student mastery. Students reaching the standard might be assigned a C, while those exceeding it by specified amounts would earn B's or

    A's. It is important that students make a direct connection between their grades and levels of learning.

b. *Use the school calendar to schedule presentation of work units.* Allow extra time for complex units and groups of students with weak skills. Avoid scheduling units of work that might be split by long school holidays. Revise the schedule continually to reflect student progress.

c. *Be responsible for the initial teaching of content.* Students are not expected to learn new material independently through worksheets, text readings, or computer programs. The teacher must present and illustrate or demonstrate what is to be learned. Use advance organizers generously.

d. *Provide for initial student practice once the material has been presented.* Include many interactive question-and-answer periods and opportunities for supervised student practice. Continue interactive practice sessions until student performance is consistent and with an acceptable error rate.

e. *Expect all students to respond to the interactive practice.* Probe, restate, and simplify questions for students making errors, and allow adequate response time. Model correct thinking strategies and response statements. Actively involve many students in the process. For example, ask each of four students to identify one cause of an effect, rather than ask one student to list four causes. Direct a fifth student to describe the analytic process used to obtain the answer and a sixth student to verify the answers of the other students. Treat errors as an inevitable part of learning a new skill, with no penalty assessed during practice.

f. *Provide students immediate and objective feedback.* Correct student errors in a nonthreatening manner before they can be practiced. An individual error can be treated as a group error, and the entire class be corrected accordingly.

g. *Provide opportunity for independent student practice.* This procedure will result in newly acquired knowledge and skills becoming firm and automatic. Effective teachers assign seatwork that is clearly explained and understood, monitor seatwork to ensure student engagement, and provide continuous feedback. Homework is begun in class to make certain everyone in the group understands what is expected. Independent practice is required until a degree of overlearning (performance above the unit standard) has been accomplished.

DETECTION   Watch for these problems:

- Behavior management plans have replaced academic learning as the classroom goal.
- Disorder and disruption are common in the classroom.
- Achievable goals have not been established.
- Students simply give up when frustrated.
- The classroom is cluttered and messy.
- Instruction is frequently interrupted.
- Students complain that work is too difficult.

The values, expectations, and beliefs of students and teachers must be carefully considered in any education program. Classrooms in which there is an emphasis upon fostering academic achievement and promoting student confidence are more successful in effective implementation of the instructional program. Inherent in this type of classroom is a climate that nurtures and challenges students.

It is the teacher's role to establish and maintain a positive learning environment that has structure, expectations, and consistent enforcement of those expectations. It is also necessary that the environment be warm and supportive, demonstrating care and concern about children. These conditions have positive effects on learning, establishing secure working conditions and building confidence in students. Maintaining a relatively low level of student anxiety is also part of the teacher's role. Student concerns should be limited to apprehension over not living up to one's potential, letting others down, or not acting in one's best interest.

●●●

An Instructional Problem

Mr. Gomez teaches seventh-grade social studies. The students in his classes are on time, sit quietly, and speak only when called upon. They always have their books, pencils, and papers ready for work when the bell rings to begin class. When a guidance counselor asked Tina what she was learning from Mr. Gomez, however, Tina replied, "Nothing. Mr. G gives extra-credit points to everybody in their seats when the bell rings. Then we are supposed to read in our books and answer the questions on the board. Every five minutes a little bell goes off, and Mr. G gives more points to everybody who is quiet with books open and writing. I just write notes to my friends cause you can get enough extra credit to pass just by sitting and not talking."

●●●

CORRECTION   Try these strategies:

1. *Focus on achievement.*

Successful classrooms are characterized by a climate that recognizes and honors academic achievement. Students clearly understand that the first classroom priority is to learn what is taught. In some cases, however, learning is replaced or given a lower position of priority.

A classroom's learning climate is the collective attitudes, beliefs, and behaviors contained within its walls. The first and most important focus of classroom activity is to impart the academic knowledge and skills necessary for students to become functioning citizens. Shifting the primary classroom focus from academic achievement to behavior management, for example, sends the message that academic achievement is less important than earning points for behaving in a specified manner.

In some classrooms there is more emphasis on the method by which instruction takes place than on achieving a learning objective. This does not mean that practicing social skills or participating in athletics should not be included in a student's school experiences. Rather, attitudes, beliefs, and activities that contribute to a positive classroom learning environment must all be subordinate to academic achievement.

Among factors that have been related to classroom climate are three that appear to have major impact. First, the climate of the school as a whole tends to shape the climate in individual classrooms. Traditional expectations of students, values held by the faculty and administration, and parent opinion place pressure on individual teachers to maintain certain classroom climates. Second, the norms of the school tend to be maintained over time, with new faculty members being socialized into prevailing behaviors. Third, the physical condition of the school and maintenance policies make specific statements about the general focus. If classrooms are shabby and English teachers don't have access to enough dictionaries, while the athletic facilities are state of the art, few will believe that academic excellence is the premier focus of the school.

Specific suggestions for increasing an emphasis on classroom achievement include:

a. *Determine lesson objectives, materials, and methods, and limit student choices to options within the framework provided by the teacher.*
b. *Present the objectives to the students.* Put them in writing, post them on the classroom wall, and send them to parents. This information is basic to a sense of purpose, organization, and self-management.
c. *Describe performance standards for the material.* Tell the students that they are expected to attain the standard and what opportunities will be provided for them to do so. Stress individual and group responsibility for learning and the work it will require.
d. *Give complete and clear directions when assigning tasks.* Keep the classroom organized and businesslike. Use good management and planning to keep interruptions to a minimum.
e. *Model an orientation toward academic achievement by being on time and prepared to teach.* Have materials ready, and maintain continuous teaching behavior. Don't merely talk about a desirable behavior if you can model it for students.
f. *Aim for a balance of high and medium success levels in student responses by varying the difficulty levels of questions.* Start, for example, with easy review questions to engage the students; then move on to more difficult questions.
g. *Chart and post the increase in student skill level to boost student motivation.* Whenever possible, have students calculate their own progress and chart it.
h. *Provide a wide variety of ways to recognize academic progress, and use them frequently.* Ribbons, buttons, stickers, certificates, and announcements can all be effective recognition for academic achievements.

•••

An Instructional Problem

Jodie Fitzwater is a warm and caring teacher. The children in her classroom know they can depend on her for assistance whenever they ask. Today, for example, Jodie was working with her lowest group of readers.

"Ms. Fitzwater? . . ." Laurie needed help to solve a seatwork problem, and so did Michael and Jeremy; J. C. needed permission to go to the bathroom; and the office secretary called on the intercom to ask for the lunch money. Jodie managed to work on reading with three of the five children in the group before it was time to send the class to art.

● ●

2. *Deal effectively with disorder and disruption.*

Classrooms in which students perform well on tests of academic achievement are usually places in which disorder is not tolerated. Before one can teach children it is necessary for them to attend and respond in an orderly manner. Children who are loud, noisy, disruptive, and inattentive are counterproductive to effective teaching. Unfortunately, many teachers tolerate these behaviors in the mistaken belief that they (a) cannot change some children, (b) should expect some children to be disruptive, or (c) have their hands tied because of potential legal liabilities over discipline.

The idealism held by beginning teachers quickly gives way to the reality of what behaviors must be controlled before learning can take place. Learning to effectively manage student behavior is the first task of becoming a teacher. Consequently, all members of a school faculty and administration should agree as to what behavior standards will be used in the classroom and school. Faculty and administrators must share equally the responsibility for enforcing the standards agreed upon, and every child should be expected to meet the standards. Should common agreement and enforcement of behavior standards in a school not be present, the individual classroom teacher still has an obligation to set and enforce behavior standards that eliminate disorder and disruption.

School discipline is controlled, to a great extent, by what teachers believe about maintaining order. A common myth that contributes to tolerating classroom disruption is that discipline problems cannot be avoided in schools within low-socioeconomic-level communities, schools with large minority populations, or urban schools. This is simply not the case. The norms for acceptable school behavior are set by the expectations and enforcement techniques of the school personnel, not the community or student population attending the school. In general, student order is greatest when (a) teachers have extensive responsibility for and contact with a reasonable number of students, (b) steps are taken to ensure adequate resources for instruction, and (c) cooperation between teachers and administrators promotes specific procedures and sanctions for disruptive behavior.

Specific suggestions for reducing disorder and disruption during instruction include:

a. *Set and enforce classroom behavior limits.* There are two stages for this—training and maintaining. When training a class, the teacher is setting and enforcing limits of behavior. Until this process is completed the students will continue to test the system and the teacher. During this period the teacher must resolve each incident, one at a time. The testing will gradually subside if the teacher is consistent, as the students accept the limits and settle into a routine. Once the students accept the standards, the teacher will occasionally have to remind the class of the limits. This usually involves a simple verbal or nonverbal cue that does not disrupt the class. A serious infraction, however, must be met with a swift and firm consequence that informs the class that the rules will be enforced.

b. *Point out student choices.* There are inevitably students who either do not stop being disruptive when confronted or repeatedly exceed the limits of acceptable behavior. Make the students realize their choice to continue misbehavior will result in a consequence that is self-inflicted. Students must (1) grasp the relation between cause and effect, (2) take responsibility for the consequences of their behavior, and (3) understand the reality of teacher expectations.

c. *Select and communicate consequences for disruptive behavior.* Consequences must be planned in advance and communicated to students. They should be reasonable, and the teacher should be capable of carrying them out. Threatening to keep a child after school, for example, may be reasonable, but if the teacher has meetings or appointments it is not a practical consequence. State the consequence in terms of the student's choice of behavior: "Latasha, since you chose not to work during math and disturbed others, you will stay after school to make up the work tomorrow. I will call your mother and inform her this afternoon." Obviously, a consequence should be something the student does not like but is not psychologically or physically harmful.

d. *Design and implement a number of incentive plans.* Incentive plans are rewards for appropriate classroom behavior and are often stronger than consequences. Pairing the two seems to strengthen both. An incentive would be to inform the class that everyone who, for two weeks, (1) completes all his or her science assignments, (2) has a daily satisfactory rating for in-seat and quiet work, and (3) demonstrates at least one daily kindness toward a classmate, will be permitted to participate in a fieldtrip to the natural science museum. A consequence would be to withhold the trip from any student who was disruptive a certain number of times within the two-week period.

e. *Designate a specific location in the classroom as an independent work area.* This area is not to be used for punishment but as an area to which a student can withdraw in order to get behavior under control. Some children who are on the verge of being out of bounds need a place to pull themselves together for a few minutes.

f. *Develop a set of contingency plans for unexpected emergencies.* Rainy days, substitutes, assemblies, schedule changes, and speakers who don't show up occur with some frequency. Planning a set of generic alternative activities can turn a potential disaster into a normal working day.

g. *Address the situation rather than the students' characteristics.* If a noisy group of students interrupts the teacher while working with a reading group, the adult's response might be, "I believe you children left your manners at home today. Now be quiet." Substitute instead, "It is so noisy that no one can get his or her work done. Let's all settle down." Another appropriate response would be to comment on the situation rather than give an order: "There is work to be completed." Dwell on what should be done, not what is wrong: "Remember, we work quietly in this room."

h. *Don't ask questions to which you know the answers.* If the teacher finds the reading center left in disarray, why ask, "Who left all these books out on the table?" when it is clear that Larry and Diane were the last two children to use the center? A better approach is to make a corrective statement: "Larry and Diane, you were the last two to use the reading center. In this room we clean up after ourselves. Please come over and put the books and headphones away."

●●●

An Instructional Problem

Carolyn Spykes has been one of the most respected teachers in her school for 10 years. When a really hard case turns up, the child is assigned to Carolyn. That was the case with Arthur, but he has proven himself impossible for even Carolyn. Arthur just doesn't care about anything. When prodded for an explanation, he shrugs his shoulders and mumbles that it doesn't matter anyway. Carolyn has not been able to get Arthur to do more than just go through the motions of being a student.

●●●

3. *Create a climate in which academic success is attainable for every student.*

A sense of futility is the perception that nothing one does will make a difference in the outcome, that trying to succeed is hopeless, that one cannot beat the system. Students who believe their behavior is futile see no reason to engage in any productive behavior because it will invariably come to nothing.

A sense of futility is different than a low self-concept. A sense of futility implies that one can have ability and desire yet consistently fail because the system does not permit success. These students are indifferent about attempting a task because the outcome is predetermined regardless of their performance. When asked, they will work on a task but see no reason for expending too much effort: No matter what they do it is not going to come out right. There is sometimes an aura of helplessness about these children.

A sense of futility is a conditioned response, built up over time, after many instances of failure. A sense of futility can be pervasive throughout a family, neighborhood, or subculture. Especially susceptible are children with little or no control over the events in their lives.

Specific suggestions for increasing the potential for every student to achieve include:

a. *Provide for choices within limits.* Permit students to choose among several ways to accomplish a required task. If they are to demonstrate a specific level of knowledge about the history of their state, for example, provide alternative ways to show that they have acquired the information. Methods of demonstrating the results of their work might include writing an original theme, writing and putting on a puppet show, giving an oral report, or taking a test.

b. *Give the students responsibility for planning and producing an academic product.* Provide an outline for the planning process, and assign students to small groups to carry it out.

c. *Pair a success-oriented student with one who has a sense of futility, and require teamwork to produce a product.* Reinforce the success-oriented student for modeling achievement, and reward the other for approximating behavior leading to achievement.

d. *Emphasize the* process *of learning, not the* product *that results.* Teach students to learn by themselves and for themselves. Help them select topics, pose questions that lead into the topic, locate resources, clarify thoughts, express conclusions, and critically examine those conclusions. The students must learn to ask questions and express, analyze, and support their own views critically and independently.

e. *Organize and use groups to help children learn to get along with others, express and receive opinions in nonthreatening ways, and make intelligent group decisions.* Facilitate by subtly guiding, reflecting, and helping to clarify feelings about self and group.

f. *Periodically require students to complete projects, long-range activities that must be organized, conducted, and reported and that require from a few days to several weeks to complete.* Work on projects contributes to building a sense of student self-determination through involvement, responsibility, and genuine accomplishment.

••

An Instructional Problem

Karen Black is a teacher in love with the sound of her own voice. When she gives directions for the day's work to her kindergarten children, she not only tells them what tasks and projects are to be completed but how, where, when, with what, and on and on. The result of her overinstruction is that the children are confused and soon drift off-task.

••

4. *Provide timely and appropriate assistance.*

As students work on assigned tasks they invariably encounter difficulties that require assistance from the teacher. Effective management of requests for assistance requires that the teacher be able to provide this help quickly while keeping the student engaged and progressing at a rate that permits completing the work on time.

Most teacher attention is given to two groups of students: those who are productive members of the class and those who are disruptive. A middle group, who provides neither great joy nor frustration, is given relatively little attention. However, students in all three groups need appropriate assistance.

Continual willingness to assist is a trait admired in everyone. Teachers are viewed positively when they manage to spread assistance to everyone in the class. Students gravitate to them, work for them, admire them, and remember them as significant influences in later years.

Assistance is a valuable commodity dependent on time, task, and teacher. A classroom in which 35 or 40 students compete for assistance from the teacher determines how much time is available for individual help. In this setting an individual student cannot be assisted as often or for as long as when fewer students are present. A learning task that is complicated and difficult will require much more assistance to all students than will a practice exercise designed to brush up on existing skills. Finally, the willingness of the teacher to become actively involved with individual students will determine the amount and quality of assistance available.

Specific suggestions for providing effective assistance to students include:

a. *Give clear, brief directions for the learning task.* Students should understand exactly what they are supposed to do, when it is to be done, and what they are to do with the completed work. Check for understanding by watching for signs of confusion, and asking one or two students to repeat the directions.

b. *Display models and reminders when several steps are to be followed or a sequence observed.* Remind the children to refer to the display before they ask for assistance from the teacher. Models and reminders posted or written on the blackboard are especially useful when students are engaged in independent work.

c. *Develop a signal system for indicating help is needed.* Students should not be encouraged to come to the teacher's desk or interrupt the teacher working with another group if they can signal the need for assistance. In addition to raising a hand, students can display a colored piece of tagboard, a token, or a simple printed sign with the message "HELP." Students should be taught to move on in the assignment or to silently read while waiting for assistance from the teacher.

d. *Move swiftly to the student needing help to avoid delays and disruptions.* Student desks and furniture should be arranged in patterns that permit ease of movement within the classroom. During independent work the teacher should be positioned in a location where he or she can observe signals for assistance and move quickly to help, circulate among the desks and tables to be close to the students, comment on work, and give help on a regular rotation.

e. *Offer the minimum amount of assistance needed to solve the problem and get students working again.* A useful sequence might be to comment positively on what the student has completed correctly and give clear directions that aid the student ("Watch the decimal," "Don't forget to borrow," "Remember your punctuation rules"). When the student has reengaged, give brief attention to the work of nearby students who have not requested assistance.

• •

An Instructional Problem

Ms. Crow's third-graders are working independently on multiplication practice sheets while she circulates, making certain that each child understands the concepts and none is practicing computation errors. It is 10:20, and morning break is scheduled for 10:30. Johnnie leaves his seat to sharpen his pencil. As he moves down the row of desks he notices a football, two basketballs, and a kickball sitting on a table next to the pencil sharpener. He approaches the table and touches the football as he passes. After sharpening his pencil, he pauses, then picks up a basketball, tosses it into the air, and catches it. Sitting at the end of the row, William notices Johnnie and signals for a pass. Johnnie obliges. Three more children stop working and join in passing the basketball while others tattle to Ms. Crow.

●●●

5. *Manage movement and materials.*

The management of movement includes how students are to enter and leave the classroom, move as individuals or in groups within the room, or move to other locations in the school. Movement management may seem trivial, but it has a large impact on student behavior and productive work habits. Inappropriate student movement causes confusion, wasted time, congestion, and disruptions. Unnecessary movement accounts directly or indirectly for a large portion of classroom discipline problems.

Classroom efficiency also depends on how well instructional materials are managed. This is especially true for how personal school supplies are obtained, used, and replaced. The objective is to store these items out of the way but readily available. It is preferable for student desks to contain items such as books, workbooks, pencils, crayons, rulers, and paper. Larger items (reference books, maps, globes) are usually kept shelved. Effective teachers attempt to keep distracting objects stored out of view and establish firm rules about movement in the classroom.

Specific suggestions for effective classroom management of movement and materials include:

a. *In the elementary grades, teach children to enter and exit the room in orderly lines.* Drawing from the seating pattern is the most efficient method for forming lines. Another effective method is to form lines based on who finishes work first, behaves best, works quietest, and so forth, using a system of reward to shape desired behavior.

b. *Give signals to indicate the kind of in-room movement expected.* For direct instruction and some seatwork, post a red card, meaning that students are to sit in their seats, work, and talk only when called upon. A yellow card means that students are to remain seated, but they may talk quietly with others during small-group work on drill and practice activities. For group and individual project work, a green card indicates that students may engage in quiet movement and talk to obtain reference materials or plan activities.

c. *Enforce a policy for pencil sharpening.* Sharpening a pencil is a necessary activity but one that can be disruptive if not properly managed. Three useful approaches include (1) setting specific times for pencil sharpening (before class begins, at a time between major study periods), (2) making sharpened pencils available to students as needed (with a limit of two or three), or (3) giving students two sharp pencils at the beginning of the day, to be kept until the end of the school day.

d. *Establish a system of passes for out-of-room movement.* Teachers should not permit students to leave the room without permission or even with permission unless absolutely necessary. Students out of the room are not engaged in learning tasks and lose valuable time. Passes have been made from wood, plastic, and metal in a variety of shapes and sizes. Clothespins have been used with primary grade children. The most effective passes, however, are formatted with space for the time and destination to be written on them. Thus, when a child leaves for the media center or bathroom, the departure time and destination are noted on the pass with a grease pencil or projection pen.

e. *Develop a system for distributing learning materials.* Suggested procedures for distribution, in preferred order, are: (1) teacher or aide distributes them before school, during recess or special subjects, or during lunch so the materials are waiting for the students, (2) monitors are trained to distribute materials during recess, lunch, or class activities as they are needed, and (3) students are instructed about location of materials and procedures for obtaining them and then expected to get their own materials as needed.

f. *Insist that children replace materials and clean up a work area after an activity is completed.* Restorage is generally done in one of four ways: (1) students themselves quietly replace the materials, (2) monitors collect and replace them, (3) students place materials in folders or baskets that are collected later by the teacher, and (4) the teacher or aide collects, organizes, and replaces the materials.

●●

An Instructional Problem

Perry's mother worked late and slept late. Consequently, Perry arrived at school from 10 to 30 minutes after the first bell, missing both breakfast and Ms. Garcia's directions to the class about the day's work. Parent conferences had produced promises to "do better," but Perry continued to be habitually late. This caused Ms. Garcia to stop an activity and give Perry directions when he arrived. By midmorning, Perry was hungry and beginning to disrupt other students' efforts to complete their assignments.

●●

6. *Manage distractions.*

Good management of normal classroom routines eliminates most of the disruptions with which teachers must cope. There are, however, a number of distracting behaviors that interfere with engaged time if teachers do not work to eliminate them.

Procrastination is the exasperating trait of putting off doing a task until the last minute. A student who has procrastinated requires teacher time and effort to get back on schedule and detracts from the orderly flow of academic performance.

Messiness is another chronic problem for some students, both in their classwork and in how they care for their materials. This annoys teachers and permits a poor work habit to become an ingrained behavior pattern.

Tattling can become an infectious disease that upsets an entire classroom. It doesn't cure itself and has many negative side effects. Students and teacher begin to focus on the negative, lose respect for each other, and expect external authority figures to resolve every dispute.

Habitual tardiness is disconcerting and annoying. Students miss important directions and information and avoid taking responsibility for themselves.

Irresponsibility refers to a general failure to get work done properly and on time; to misuse or mistreat materials, equipment, and facilities; and to live up to ordinary expectations.

Specific suggestions for coping with these classroom distractions include:

a. *Reduce procrastination.*
   • Keep instructional tasks as short as possible while still attaining the learning objective.
   • Break long tasks down into a series of shorter elements, and state a deadline for each.
   • Emphasize deadlines. For short, in-class tasks, occasionally call out the time remaining for work.
   • Pair an incentive with completion of a task. Inform a student, for example, that when finished, he or she may have time on the computer.
b. *Reward neatness.*
   • Schedule group discussions about pride in self, schoolwork, and the classroom. Illustrate the link between pride and neatness.
   • Post and reward neatest papers and tidiest work areas.
   • Implement a reward system for neat schoolwork and a clean work area.
c. *Discourage needless tattling.*
   • Discuss the nature of tattling, its bad side effects, and why students should resolve conflict independently.
   • Establish a classroom rule that the teacher will listen only to tales wherein one's rights have been seriously violated. Define *seriously* with the students.

- Insist the tattler put the complaint in writing and add a suggestion for eliminating the problem.
- Direct the tattler to make the complaint at recess, lunch, or some other time when it can be considered carefully and seriously.

d. *Decrease tardiness.*
- Discuss with the class their responsibilities and roles in coming to school. Be certain they all understand the importance of being to school on time.
- Make the daily opening activities so attractive, enjoyable, and important that students will feel left out if they miss them.
- Set up rewards for punctuality and punishment for tardiness. Have the students assist in selecting the rewards and punishments.

e. *Teach responsibility.*
- Periodically discuss with students what responsibility means in the classroom, how it contributes to the good of the group, and what is expected of each student.
- Assign specific responsibilities to each student as his or her part in managing the classroom.
- Have the students evaluate their own behavior on points related to responsibility (punctuality, completing work, care of materials, neatness of work area, helping others), and use contracts for future improvement.

●●

An Instructional Problem

Michael is one of those quiet seventh-graders that teachers worry about. When the rest of the group is whooping with laughter, Michael manages a chuckle or two. When the class is engaged in a lively classroom discussion, he will answer a factual question if called upon but will never volunteer. He rarely completes assignments and generally explains by saying "It was too hard for me" or "I can't do that stuff."

●●

7. *Foster accurate self-evaluation by students.*

A student's self-assessment of ability to work and learn can function as a self-fulfilling prophecy. In this process, children often make an unsubstantiated judgment that they have low ability to learn and expect evaluation to verify that as fact. Subsequent classroom behavior based on the distorted self-evaluation convinces the child that his or her original perception was correct.

In this instance, the self-fulfilling prophecy has two parts: the inaccurate self-assessment and the process that confirms the false assumption. Both may be unconscious, which makes the student behavior sequence difficult to break. Unfortunately, the same mechanism can operate at the group level, as well as with an individual. A group within a class, a class, a grade level, or an entire school may be victimized by the cycle.

Low concept of academic ability usually results from many small but consistent actions, leading to cumulative results. Over time the effects build up; later distorted judgments are strengthened by earlier ones. Some forces in society that differentiate and evaluate are so strong that it may be impossible to get a value-free judgment of ability.

Specific suggestions for fostering accurate student self-evaluation include:

a. *Break the teaching unit into many small units that have starting and ending points.* Children with low self-concepts, who doubt their academic ability, need to begin and successfully complete many work units in order to believe that they can be achievers.

b. *Post progress charts to provide tangible feedback to students.* Low-self-concept students must be frequently reminded that they are making progress and completing academic work. A progress chart clearly illustrates how much (or how accurately) work is being completed.

c. *Reward satisfactory work habits often.* The key to achieving is to complete tasks assigned. Academic work is more likely to be completed if a child has good work habits. Frequently praise or reward coming to class promptly, staying seated, being on task, and having the school supplies necessary to complete academic work.

d. *Tell students about a peer's successful academic performance.* Deliberately allow the praise to be overheard by several students, including (when possible) the one who is the topic of discussion. Comments made to a student's peers can be a powerful medium for changing self-perception.

e. *Model how to praise individuals for academic effort and work behaviors.* Reinforce students who praise or make positive comments about their peers' academic performance. When the entire class is encouraged to make these statements, a positive atmosphere is created in which students begin to believe in their ability to perform.

f. *Whenever possible tell other adults about a student's successful academic performance.* Deliberately allow the praise to be overheard by several adults and students, including (when feasible) the student who is the topic of discussion. Prompt other teachers to comment on the student's work. The more a child hears he or she is capable of success, the more likely he or she is to believe it.

g. *Prepare a display and select a "Student of the Week," based on work performance.* Post the child's picture, a brief biography, and award a privilege or two. Children with low self-concepts will be encouraged and pleased.

h. *Call parents and inform them of how well their child is achieving in the classroom.* Ask the parents to praise the child, as well, prompting them as to what and how to present the message if necessary.

CHAPTER 8
DEVELOPING AN EFFECTIVE DISCIPLINE PLAN

DETECTION   Watch for these problems:

- Students do not follow directions and are unable to demonstrate exactly the expected classroom routine.
- Students fail to respond to teacher requests.
- Students lack self-control over academics and classroom conduct.
- Students lack a clear understanding of teacher expectations.
- Strategies for decreasing or eliminating inappropriate student behavior are sometimes misunderstood.

It sometimes appears that nothing less than sorcery is needed to establish and maintain a well-organized and smoothly operating classroom. Teachers are challenged daily to instruct students with diverse abilities, suppress attempts by some to disrupt that instruction, and maintain a climate conducive to learning and positive social interaction. In attempting to detect and correct shortcomings in current practices, general case strategies (i.e., procedures with broad applicability) that have been proven effective are presented. Emphasis is on a group-individualized approach to classroom discipline that is aimed at preventing problems before they occur.

CORRECTION   Try these strategies:

1. *Script out classroom routines.*

Some authorities recommend and many teachers attest to the usefulness of classroom scripts, consisting of step-by-step written accounts of various student behaviors. Scripting out the classroom routine is advocated for dealing with events that occur regularly: student submission of class assignments, responses to teacher requests, use of time out, student requests for teacher assistance, and so on. The script becomes a permanent product that can be easily reintroduced to the same or new students. As a written record of classroom standards, it evokes less antagonism than repeated teacher verbal directions (e.g., "nag statements).

In producing a script of a particular classroom routine, first conduct a behavior analysis in order to detect the necessary and sufficient steps that comprise the desired behavior. Next, compose a simulated teacher-student dialogue and devise accompanying role-play exercises for students to repeatedly engage in the behavior. Finally, establish a system for rewarding exemplary pupil performance (e.g., no homework that evening).

Use of scripts combined with behavioral rehearsal is well suited to the installation of various discipline policies. An example is training students to engage in selected time-out procedures to decrease unwanted behavior. Time out (defined as the contingent loss of positive reinforcement for a specified period) is imposed during moments of conflict and tension. Rarely will a student be able to respond appropriately to an unfamiliar request at such a critical time (e.g., nonseclusionary time out consisting of removal from an art activity). However, a script that contains training exercises that cover exactly what behavior is expected increases significantly the likelihood of student compliance. Table 8.1 illustrates a script devised to instruct students in the use of time out.

TABLE 8–1   Sample Script on Time Out

TEACHER	STUDENTS
"I'd like to talk to you about some ways of dealing with being upset. Has anyone ever been really frustrated over not being able to do an arithmetic problem?"	"I have."
"What did you do?"	"I think I threw away the paper."
"I've got another one. How about being angry because I didn't call on you when you knew the answer to a question?"	"That's happened to me a few times."
"Ok, Jim, what did you do?"	"I yelled at you and left the room. Sorry."

TABLE 8–1   Sample Script on Time Out (continued)

TEACHER	STUDENTS
"Remember our class rule about staying in control?" When you lose control you stop learning and usually make it impossible for others to do their work."	"That's about respecting the rights of others, isn't it?"
"It sure is! So, if I see that you are having a big problem handling a particular situation, I will tell you that you must start work immediately or take a time out."	"What do you mean, take a time out?"
"Good question. You must take a time out when you do something that is unacceptable—like disrupt group instruction. Ordinarily, I will tell you to move to the chair in the back of the room for two minutes. After two minutes have passed, *if* you are in control, *then* you should quietly rejoin the group. But *if* you have not calmed down, *then* I will extend the time out another two minutes. Nancy, can we practice taking a time out?"	"OK."
"Nancy, I'd like you to pretend to be upset."	"That's easy."
"Nancy, kicking your deks is disrupting class. You need to begin work right now."	[Nancy continues to kick.]
"That's not being in control. Take a time out on the chair." [Statement is made in a matter-of-fact tone.]	[Nancy leaves the group and sits on the chair.]
The two minutes is over, Nancy. I'm glad you calmed down and are back in control. That was a very good decision. OK, Jim, how about you?"	

2. *Use peers to prompt appropriate behavior.*

Much has been written about the fact that most school-aged students can function successfully as change agents and can positively influence peers' behavior. Support for casting students in the role of change agent is linked to several factors. First, adult-controlled discipline programs often fail to achieve long lasting gains in improved behavior. Second, students are able to positively influence classmates' behavior in a variety of situations even when an adult is not present. Third, classmates acting as change agents can serve as models of appropriate behavior. Finally, peer intervention is actually preferred by many students over that of an adult.

Many studies have used students to promote desirable behavior among classmates (e.g., social skills training). Less attention has been given to student-initiated efforts to (a) correct negative behavior exhibited by classmates and (b) make students aware of the impact of their behavior on others.

A corrective strategy that combines teacher direction with peer participation is peer challenge. Each time a target student engages in an inappropriate act, the teacher asks the student's peers to respond to the following questions: (a) "Karen seems to be having a problem. Who can tell her what the problem is?" (b) "Can you tell Karen why that is a problem?" (c) "Who can tell Karen what she needs to do to solve the problem?" The teacher verbally reinforces those students who respond positively to these questions/prompts. Further, both the teacher and Karen's classmates verbally and gesturally reinforce the target student for accepting and following the recommendations. In applying the peer-challenge strategy, the teacher does not relinquish all external control and is supportive of meaningful changes in target student behavior that approximate the final goal.

●●

An Instructional Problem

Ms. Hunter lamented that her students appeared to think that they had little control over academic productivity. No matter what they did, the work was always the same. This sense of helplessness diminished the amounts of effort and enthusiasm exhibited by the students.

●●

3. *Use goal setting for self-control.*

In recent years, a proliferation of studies have examined children's self-control, and the results have often been striking. Indeed, evidence shows that self-control procedures can produce changes in a wide range of academic performance and maladaptive classroom behavior. One way of promoting student self-control is to institute goal setting. The following dialogue illustrates how goal setting can be introduced into daily classroom operation:

It's time to get ready for our class meeting. Please put your work in your folders, and put away all folders and workbooks. Remember, the rules are: 1) you need to stay in your seat; 2) talk only when I call on you by name; and 3) everyone must tell the truth. As you know, the reason for our meeting is to choose a goal to work on to learn more each day and to be successful in school. We will also review whether each of you reached your goal for today. (If you do not participate or are unable to follow the rules, you must leave the group and sit by yourself.). Melissa, will you tell us the goals that lead to good learning? Thank you. Now I'm going to ask each of you in turn to tell everyone your goal and to say whether you were able to make that goal or not. Remember, you need to explain exactly what you did to reach your goal. Rebecca, let's begin with you . . .

Goals are stated positively and in enough detail that their occurrence (versus nonoccurrence) can be easily distinguished by students and adults. A goal-setting session usually takes place in the morning; a review session usually occurs at the end of the school day, after the class period in which goal setting was used.

The following examples illustrate what might constitute attainment or nonattainment:

Attaining Goal—The student is engaged in responses appropriate to instruction: calculating problems on math sheet; eyes on sheet; looks at teacher if giving directions or answering student's question. *Attaining* is recorded if the student is using a number line or other means for obtaining answers.

Not Attaining Goal—The student is not engaged for at least three seconds and is talking to peers, staring out the window, scanning the classroom, playing with toys, and so on. Some teachers establish the criterion that if the student is attaining his or her goal, a number of slashmarks is entered beside the student's name. The frequency of slashes (under each category) serves as the basis for teacher feedback on student attainment during the review session.

a. *Add self-monitoring.* For many students it is advantageous to incorporate a self-monitoring component to goal setting. For that purpose, with younger students, "countoons" on 5" x 8" cards might consist of: (a) the student's name, (b) a picture of a happy face (signifying goal attainment), and (c) a frowning face (indicating nonattainment). A tally is maintained by the student who is signaled when to record. Figure 8–1 presents an example of the "countoon."

In contrast, for older students it may be enough to instruct them simply to record a slashmark in a box on their work at the designated times if they are attaining their goal. Once trained, students can be signaled by means of a minute-meter timer. The timer should be set (and reset) on a variable interval basis. This way, students are unable to predict precisely when the timer will ring. The number of slashes recorded by each student and independently confirmed through teacher observation can serve as the basis of teacher-student and student-student evaluation during the review session.

b. *Shift program administration.* As appealing as the use of some student-control strategies may be, a major drawback of their use is

FIGURE 8–1 Sample "Countoon"

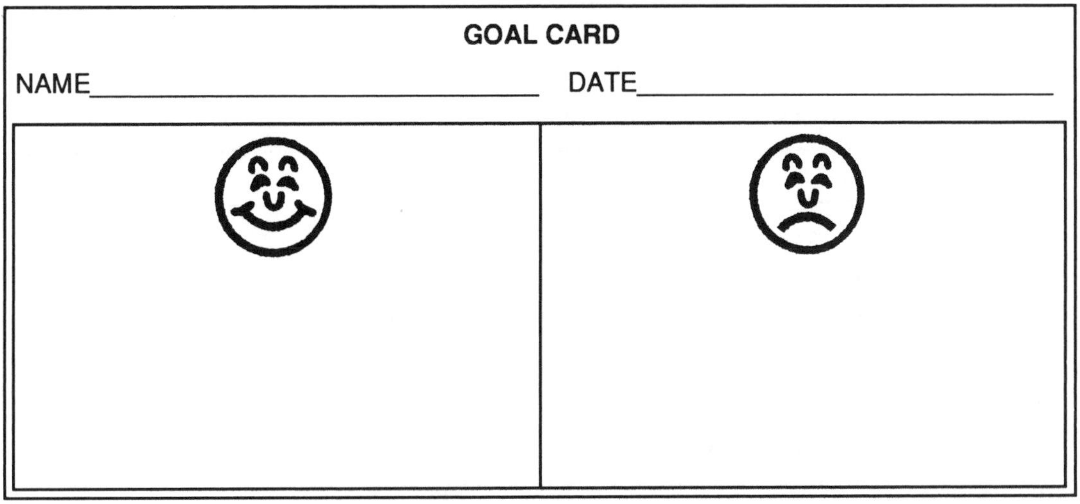

GOAL CARD

NAME_____   DATE_____

the uncertainty that surrounds the shift from adult to student control. One way of offsetting this problem is to gradually but systematically shift program administration. In instituting such a program, first the adult not only determines the classroom objective (i.e., the academic task to be performed) but also selects and administers the reinforcer (see Figure 8–2). By comparison, the student is required simply to comply with the specified instructional arrangement. In succeeding phases, determination of the reinforcer and then the academic task shifts from teacher to student. By observing the step-by-step shift to student control, the teacher can evaluate the impact at each stage of the program. The pace at which transfer of control occurs for each student can be individually determined.

●●

An Instructional Problem

Ms. Waters, the assistant principal, walked into the classroom at the worst possible moment. Mr. Lewis, a first-year teacher, looked bewildered and upset. In attempting to punish two or three students for calling out, he had succeeded in creating more conflict. Even some of the students who ordinarily behaved looked uncertain about expectations.
●●

FIGURE 8–2   Five Steps toward Shifting Control

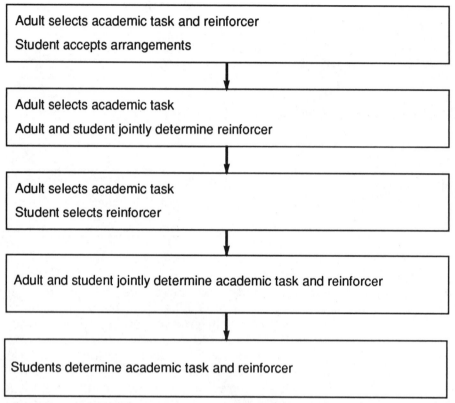

Source: Adapted from Reitz, A., Gable, R. A., & Trout, B. A. (1984). Education for self-control: Classroom applications of group process procedures. In R. B. Rutherford, Jr., & C. M. Nelson (Eds.) *Monograph in Behavioral Disorders* (Vol. VII). Reston, VA: Council for Exceptional Children. Reprinted by permission.

4. *Establish classroom rules.*

Establishing rules is a useful means of communicating expected and appropriate behavior to students. Well-designed rules that are publicly posted and to which teachers routinely refer when dispensing positive feedback will clarify policies and thus reduce discipline problems. Rule selection is usually linked to class discussion of factors that shape the climate for learning and socialization.

a. *State behavior positively.* Initiated by the teacher, classroom conversation centers on behavior stated in the positive (e.g., "Raise your hand to signal a need for assistance."). During the course of this exchange, a preliminary list of 10 to 15 general rules is consolidated into 4 to 5 well-defined classroom rules. (Some of the rules plus additional rules may be established for other settings, e.g., cafeteria, playground, library). Here is a list of common classroom rules:

- Respect the rights and property of others.
- Pay attention to the teacher and to your work.
- Raise your hand to talk or to seek assistance.
- Settle disagreements by staying in control and talking to reach a solution.

b. *List examples and nonexamples.* Next, a corresponding list is created of multiple examples (along with nonexamples) of observable behavior that exemplifies rule compliance. This step is important because these examples (and nonexamples) represent the exact responses students will be trained to perform.

c. *Implement training exercises.* Through a series of training exercises, each student is given the opportunity not only to specify verbally but also to perform and obtain feedback on the desired behavior. In addition, classmates are asked to label each example or nonexample according to the appropriate rule (e.g., respecting the rights and property of others). Positive and regular practice of classroom rules (repeated daily at the beginning and occasionally thereafter) helps ensure that students will grasp the concept of each rule and be able to comply with rule-governed expectations.

d. *Establish consequences for rule violations.* Use of scripts and practice exercises is strongly recommended to put into place a hierarchy of consequences for rule violations. Decisions should be tempered by the magnitude of the infraction—its duration and intrusiveness into overall class routine. Very intense student acts (e.g., physical aggression) may lead to immediate imposition of more severe penalties than listed below (e.g., exclusionary time out).

1st violation—private verbal warning
2nd violation—nonexclusionary time out
3rd violation—time out coupled with loss of recess for three days

5. *Use punishment sparingly.*

In most cases, use of positive strategies is recommended (e.g., praise, student contracts, group contingencies). Even so, application of positive options will not always suffice. Judicious use of punishment (defined as an event that follows a student behavior and decreases its strength or probability of recurrence) can be an effective component of a sound discipline plan. Several techniques that are only mildly aversive are discussed.

a. *Use time outs judiciously.* Teachers faced with a range of disruptive classroom acts need to know about reduction techniques as a management tool. Time out may be instituted in several forms. It may consist of the temporary removal of student access to classroom

reinforcers (e.g., the teacher collects flashcards a student is reviewing with a peermate). By comparison, a more intrusive form of time
out can be exclusionary, as when a student is physically removed
from the immediate setting (e.g., directed to take a two-minute chair
time out). A note of caution is necessary regarding the use of
exclusionary time out. Apart from the importance of adhering to
strict guidelines for its use, more restrictive forms of time out
eliminate virtually all opportunity for student learning. An effective
reduction technique that may be preferable consists of teacher
reinforcement of either specific student responses that are incompatible with the target behavior (e.g., hand raising rather than calling
out) or all other acceptable behavior.

b. *Verbal reprimand.* A common punishment associated with teacher
verbal behavior is the reprimand. Disapproval statements that
clearly specify the target behavior, justify its unacceptability, and
center on a single behavior can be highly effective.

c. *Consider response cost.* In addition, teachers should consider the
use of response cost. Used singly or in connection with token reinforcement, a response cost functions as a punishment imposed
following an inappropriate act (e.g., loss of a letter grade for spelling
errors or playground access due to an episode of physical aggression). Simply put, a student's engagement in an unwanted behavior
leads to its "costing something," as natural an extension of the
violation as possible.

d. *Avoid overdependence on inappropriate punishment.* Because of its
relative effectiveness in eliminating a wide range of unwanted behavior, teachers sometimes unwittingly become too dependent on the
use of punishment. In fact, punishment may reinforce the punisher.
As with any strategy, flaws exist in the application of punishment.
For example, a response cost should still allow a student to recoup
a portion of what was lost (e.g., half the points lost for stealing can
be regained by returning the object in question). Further, teacher
reprimands may be wrongly delivered in general terms and with a
negative intonation. Classroom suspension is sometimes indiscriminately proposed as a misapplication of time out. It is enough to say
that care must be exercised in using reduction strategies, and
replacement behavior should always be promoted when attempting
to eliminate an unwanted behavior.

e. *Corporal punishment.* Another serious consideration involves the use
of corporal punishment. While there is certainly a precedent for the
use of corporal punishment in public schools, serious ethical and
legal considerations may mitigate its application. State law and
school district regulations must be carefully examined before using
corporal punishment.

At an even more fundamental level, corporal punishment may be so humiliating to the student that it fosters a problematic instructional environment. Moreover, the use of corporal punishment may produce a view of the teacher that is less than desirable, create a model for the rectification of student problems, and preclude the use of less coercive and more positive approaches. In short, corporal punishment is at best a means of last resort that may harm the teacher as well as the student.

CHAPTER 9
CREATING AN ORDERLY SETTING FOR LEARNING

DETECTION

Watch for these problems:

- The classroom environment is crowded, distracting, and messy.
- The classroom environment lacks structure.
- The students do not know where to find materials.
- The students exhibit noisy, disruptive behavior.
- Classroom activities are not carried out efficiently.

Creating an orderly setting is the first step in establishing an environment that is conducive to learning and to preventing behavior problems. An orderly and attractive environment can have a very positive effect on behavior by improving the level and quality of student interactions. This in turn can help the teacher and students carry out daily activities efficiently without excessive noise or disruption.

This chapter provides guidelines for the physical layout of a classroom, including an efficient room plan for areas, furniture, and equipment for specific activities and appropriate use of wall, ceiling, and floor space. Also included are guidelines for management of daily activities within the setting: student movement, seating positions, personal space, individual duties, and daily routines. The chapter ends with adjustments that can be made to facilitate the changing needs of students and teachers.

• •

An Instructional Problem

Ms. Truman's classroom has all the elements of a very disorderly environment. It is crowded with an assortment of furniture she has acquired from garage sales each Saturday. Materials are scattered everywhere, and most of the students do not know where to find what they need. Areas have not been designated for specific activities, and students move their desks around as they please. Even the bulletin boards and walls are cluttered with a chaotic mixture of student work, classroom rules, posters, and other displays. The disorderly nature of the room spills over into the behavior of the students; an ever increasing amount of inappropriate behavior is exhibited daily.

• •

CORRECTION   Try these strategies:

1. *Carefully arrange the physical layout.*

   It is important to plan the physical layout of the classroom very carefully, designating areas for specific activities, determining furniture to include and arranging it, decorating areas for different purposes, and organizing teaching and student materials for easy access. Figures 9–1 and 9–2 are examples of two possible physical layouts. Depending on the size of the classroom and type of class (regular class, special class, etc.), several areas may be designated for specific activities.

   a. *Structure the large-group area.* Before arranging desks and other areas of the classroom, determine first where large-group instruction will take place. The large group is not usually appropriate for individual specific skill instruction but may be appropriate for such activities as discussion of current events, show-and-tell, science experiments, and preparing for a special class event. It may be helpful to place this area near a chalkboard, an electrical outlet, and an extra table to hold supplies and equipment.

   b. *Create small-group areas.* Small groups are formed based on common needs and are appropriate for teaching new skills and conducting reading and math groups. In small groups of three to five, students tend to participate more and are less likely to exhibit behavior problems. Small-group instruction may take place at a table, on a rug in a designated area of the room, or in a semicircle of desks facing the teacher. It should be in an area of the room that is relatively free from noise and distraction.

   c. *Provide individual student areas.* Each student needs a place to call his or her own, to store personal materials, and to sit during individual or group activities. Each student will either have a personal place at a small table or be assigned a desk. Careful attention to seating arrangements is important to an efficiently run classroom. Students who are highly distractible may need a very private area, like a study carrel, or be placed close to the teacher area or away from certain other students. If a student is placed in a carrel, it should be presented as a positive place to learn and not confused with a time-out area.

   d. *Organize a teacher area.* If the classroom teacher decides to have an area in the classroom for his or her desk, it should be kept well organized and decorated in an attractive manner. Additionally, the teacher's desk should be placed in a location that will allow broad visibility by everyone in the classroom. A student chair may be placed next to the teacher's desk, a "chair of honor" or "chair of distinction," to be used for individual conferences or one-to-one instruction.

e. *Establish a paraprofessional/volunteer work area.* If the classroom is large enough, a work space for paraprofessionals and volunteers is helpful. They will appreciate having a special space to prepare materials or work with individual or small groups of students. This area may also be used for special student helpers (peer tutors or students who have completed their work early) to prepare materials or work with other students. This area should be situated across the room from the teacher area to allow additional monitoring of the classroom. A list of activities may be placed on a nearby bulletin board, including tasks for the volunteer to complete.

f. *Develop a recreation area.* A reinforcement area may be placed away from individual and small-group areas for use as a rewarding place for students who have completed their work. This area may have a couch or comfortable chairs, beanbag chairs, a loft, an area rug, books and magazines, a record player or tape recorder with head-phones, games, and the like.

g. *Equip an audiovisual area.* Set up a separate center for audiovisual equipment if there is enough space in the classroom. In this area, a

FIGURE 9–1 Physical Layout of Room, Plan A

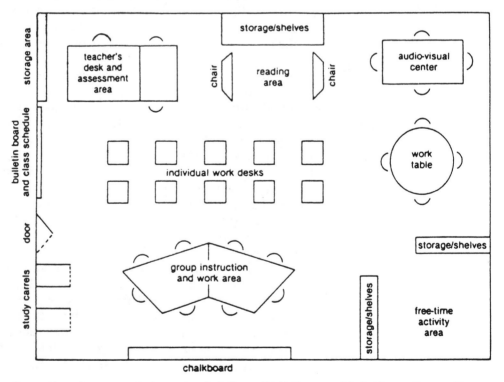

Source: From *Assessment for instruction,* S. S. Evans, W. H. Evans, and C. D. Mercer (Boston: Allyn and Bacon, 1986). Copyright 1986 by Allyn and Bacon. Rjeprinted by permission.

computer, tape recorder, language master, VCR, or overhead projector may be used by individuals or small groups of students.

h. *Arrange specific purpose areas.* Additional areas of the classroom may be used for various purposes, depending on the needs of the students and teacher:

- a time-out area, which may be a priority for certain situations;
- built-in cubbies or separate containers for students to store lunchboxes and other school materials;
- learning centers placed in corners of the classroom or near bulletin boards or chalkboards;
- self-correction stations, a classroom library, or materials/ storage centers;
- cabinet tops to display science or history projects, a globe, instructional kits (e.g., SRA materials);
- shelf space reserved for particular textbooks and reference books;
- cabinet space for equipment and other supplies that are off limits to the students or are not used often.

FIGURE 9–2 Physical Layout of Room, Plan B

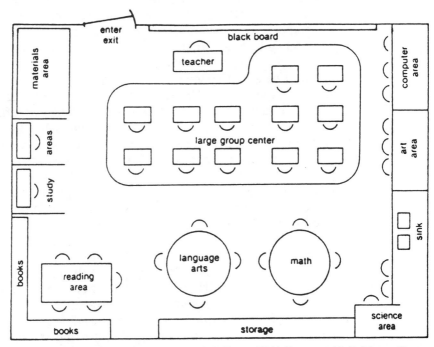

Source: From *Assessment for instruction,* S. S. Evans, W. H. Evans, and C. D. Mercer (Boston: Allyn and Bacon, 1986). Copyright 1986 by Allyn and Bacon. Reprinted by permission.

Teaching and student materials and supplies should be organized and labeled for easy access and located where they will be most functional. Various types and uses for equipment are discussed in Chapter 12.

i. *Define each area.* Designated areas of the classroom may be divided and then changed as needed by using such devices as movable partitions and lightweight screens, including chalkboards or bulletin boards, bookshelves, file cabinets, study carrels, or coatracks. Facing student desks in different directions will also help redefine the room, as will the use of area rugs. Dividing the room in this way will allow for different types of activities and structure or flexibility when needed.

j. *Use resources.* Bulletin boards and other wall and ceiling space may be used to display work or materials, post class rules, provide schedules and feedback charts, list daily assignments, highlight new skills, or instruct (e.g., steps to complete a research paper). These areas and displays should be visually appealing; catch the students' interests with current events, trends, or themes; be uncluttered; and changed frequently. If possible, the students should be involved in designing the various areas.

Usually, furniture has already been purchased and placed in each classroom, but occasionally funds will be available for new furniture for a classroom in a new school, for example. It is important to consider the quality, size, function, and price of the furniture. In some settings, it is possible to contract with the local education agency to have furniture built to specifications.

2. *Arrange seating and personal space constructively.*

As previously noted, the teacher's desk should face the students and allow broad visibility of the classroom and all students. Student desks or tables may be arranged in a variety of ways. It is important that young children have many opportunities for language development and small-group interaction. Therefore, children in preschool or early-elementary grades are often seated in small groups at tables or desks arranged to promote language interaction. In the upper-elementary grades, it is more common to see desks arranged in double or single rows. In the middle and high school grades, it is also common to see desks arranged in single rows.

Seating position can also affect interaction and attention to the lesson and teacher. Students seated in the center and front often have more interaction with the teacher; this in turn may affect student performance. Teachers should be certain that students can easily see instructional presentations and the chalkboard without craning their necks. The teacher should change the seating arrangement occasionally to make sure all students have the opportunity to sit next to a variety of peers and in a variety of places. It is also important that the teacher circulate around the classroom often, moving easily among students to give help quickly and ensure the most effective learning environment. The seating arrangement can also facilitate independent or interactive activities:

a. *Encourage on-task behavior.* More distance between students generally leads to increased levels of on-task behavior. Low-performing students or students with behavior problems are often seated near the teacher's desk, at an individual study carrel, at the front of the room, or isolated from the other students. If possible, students with academic or social problems should be seated for a clear view of selected peers who model appropriate academic and social behavior.

b. *Facilitate cooperative learning activities.* Seating arrangements and portability of desks and tables can facilitate cooperative learning opportunities. Flexibility should be built in to allow students to work together on projects, assist one another, and share experiences and knowledge.

3. *Efficiently manage movement and routines.*

Effectively managing movement and planning individual student duties and daily routines are also important elements of an efficiently run classroom. Students who are constantly moving around the room may distract others and in general are not on-task. Undesirable behaviors, such as hitting and loud talking, are sometimes associated with students who are constantly out-of-seat, roaming the classroom. Care must be taken, however, not to impose a rigid system that requires all students to constantly sit in their seats. Rather, individual initiative and curiosity should be fostered while encouraging personal responsibility. It is important for the classroom teacher to remember that learning can occur in as well as out of the student's seat. The goal of instructional management, therefore, is not merely to force students to sit but to ensure that an effective educational program is delivered when students are in their seats.

Classroom routine can do a great deal to establish a pattern of appropriate and productive behavior. Students and teachers alike function much more efficiently when they know what to expect and when to expect it. Too much routine, however, can produce a deadly monotony in which the excitement and exuberance of learning is slowly but surely pulverized. When this happens a routine becomes a rut, and dissatisfaction and lethargy set in.

The goal is to recognize that instructional management techniques that reduce student movement and foster routines are but tools to be used in implementing the educational program. Their utility is in helping, not handcuffing, the classroom teacher and student.

a. *Plan for traffic control.* Since strategies for dealing with student movement are detailed in Chapter 7, only a few are mentioned here. It is important that the high-traffic areas in the classroom be free of congestion. Traffic patterns should be considered when deciding on locations of the pencil sharpener, self-correcting stations, the teacher's desk, and materials that will be used frequently. To ensure that a classroom will be free of congestion, rules or a pass system may be established (e.g., one student at a time) for using the pencil sharpener, the drinking fountain, the restrooms, and the sink. Other rules may be appropriate to ensure an orderly physical setting, such as appointing a line leader for the day or week and assigning classroom helpers to clean chalkboards and erasers, pass out and collect materials, lead the Pledge of Allegiance, feed the fish, water the plants, correct papers, and assemble materials.

b. *Establish routines.* Teachers will learn to use effective techniques, such as correcting work while circulating around the classroom; allowing the quiet row or table to line up first; and establishing routines for the beginning, transition periods, and ending of the day. For example, at the beginning of the day, students may be asked to check the chalkboard for a morning assignment, hand in homework, or continue work on a specific project. When returning to the classroom from lunch or recess, students should go right to their desks, read or rest, and use the restrooms and water fountain one at a time. At the end of the day, a routine may be established for cleaning and straightening various areas of the room and desks, arranging materials to go home, and leaving on time without confusion. This will end the day on a positive note and prompt enthusiasm for returning the next day.

4. *Adjust arrangements as needed.*

Student as well as teacher needs are constantly changing. What was needed and appropriate at one time may be unnecessary at another. Even the best formulated plan will be in need of modification as students learn and classroom conditions change. Therefore, the classroom teacher must recognize when change is needed and implement the change in a timely manner.

a. *Discover the problem.* Careful observation should serve to discover the time, place, and individuals involved with the instructional problem. What may seem to be a very generalized problem may be related to a specific time of the day, area of the room, instructional activity, or a particular student. For example, crowding around the water fountain may only be a problem related to recess and particularly on hot days. As a result, it may not be necessary to institute a large-scale intervention but rather one that solves the specific problem.

b. *Consider possible solutions.* Making a sketch of the problem area in the classroom is always a good first step. It may suggest a variety of alternatives, such as changing traffic patterns, the location of a learning center, student seating, or scheduling. Often, however, an obvious change is not apparent. In these cases, ideas for change can come from fellow teachers, students, professional literature, and observation of student preferences and needs. Before instituting a change, the classroom teacher must carefully consider if the proposed alteration will create new and possibly unanticipated problems. For example, changing the placement of bookshelves may solve a traffic flow difficulty but create a worse problem by making the reading books less accessible.

Not every problem necessitates an intervention. A new piece of audiovisual equipment, a new learning center, or a novel and interesting item in the classroom generally sparks a great deal of student interest and attention. In these and other cases, a general intervention is not appropriate. What is necessary, however, is time management, so that all students can see and experience the item of interest, and patience by the teacher, who knows that the novelty will eventually wear off.

c. *Institute and evaluate the change.* The students' as well as the teacher's behavior should be carefully evaluated to determine the effect of the intervention. It may be necessary to further refine the intervention to meet the particular instructional needs.

DETECTION   Watch for these problems:

- The classroom environment lacks structure.
- The teacher has not developed an appropriate schedule.
- The teacher does not adhere to a regular schedule.
- Students do not know what they are supposed to do.
- Students never seem to get everything done.
- The teacher does not deal effectively with paperwork.

How teachers and students manage time has much to do with their success in the classroom. Time is a valuable resource that if used efficiently and appropriately can result in student learning and achievement. In fact, student achievement in school is closely related to the amount of time spent actively engaged in appropriate academic activities. Teachers who obtain poor achievement from students frequently use too much class time for noninstructional activities and/or for non-interactive tasks.

●●

An Instructional Problem

Ms. Litner is a resource room teacher who works with students with learning problems. Students come to her classroom for about an hour each day for help with reading, language arts, or math. Although Ms. Litner has a schedule posted on her bulletin board, she has trouble adhering to it. She has recruited many volunteers to help in her classroom—parents, grandparents, other school-aged students, and practicum students from the university. Ms. Litner likes to try every new approach that comes along, so she has many materials and equipment that she has purchased and many teacher-made materials that she has developed. Ms. Litner is also a very energetic teacher who is always changing her bulletin boards and room arrangement so her students never know what to expect or where to find their desks or materials when they enter her room. Students who come into her room at their scheduled time usually wander around, waiting for someone to tell them what to do first, next, and so on.

Friday is party day in Ms. Litner's class. The students can bring a friend and play games during their scheduled time. Although Ms. Litner stays very busy and her students seem to like her, by the end of Friday, Ms. Litner is usually exhausted and wondering just what she has accomplished during the week.

●●●

Teachers vary widely in how they allocate time. Sometimes they do not realize how time is actually spent until they analyze it in detail. Teachers must develop schedules that allot time for various classes and activities during the school day. Moreover, they must adhere to the schedule as much as possible.

●●●

An Instructional Problem

Ms. Klugman was an expert at math. She had studied to be an architect but changed her mind and decided to become a teacher. Her students loved math, too, because Ms. Klugman made the class so much fun. During one math period, the students measured the building and all the rooms in the school and made drawings to scale. They learned to make bar graphs and pie charts and were experts in the metric system. However, Ms. Klugman's class spent so much time with math activities that language arts, science, and social studies were often neglected.

●●●

CORRECTION   Try these strategies:

1. *Establish a daily schedule.*
   The daily schedule should reflect the maximum time for instruction in every content area; activities should be selected to offer the greatest teaching and learning potential. As much as possible, tasks and goals should be selected that can be taught and evaluated directly.

   a. *Allocate time.* Time should be allocated for activities based on their importance. Usually, these activities will have to be scheduled between special classes (music, art, and P.E.), which have been assigned in advance. The time allocated for various activities and subject areas may be based on guidelines recommended by a state department of education. These guidelines attempt to balance various areas of the curriculum by recommending percentages of time to be spent in specific content areas (for example, 40% of the day for language arts, 15% for math, etc.). However, this approach assumes that all students need the same amount of time for certain activities and subject areas and does not leave much room for individualization.

b. *Designate key time slots.* Generally, the most important activities of the day (language arts and math) are scheduled when students are at their peak levels of functioning, usually in the morning. Science and social studies activities are frequently scheduled in the afternoon; it is important that these periods are structured to compensate for lower levels of student alertness by requiring more student participation, more hands-on tasks, and so on. A sample daily class schedule is presented in Figure 10-1.

c. *Provide flexibility.* If possible, flexibility should be built into the schedule to allow for variations in learning. If some students are having difficulty in math, for example, they can receive more math time either during the math period or at another time. To accomplish individualization, a schedule should first be established and then revised for each student as necessary. Time should be set aside for the teacher, paraprofessional, or volunteer to work with individual students having difficulty. Also, if possible, everyone, including students who are not having problems, should have an opportunity to work with the teacher individually at times during the week. (See Chapter 11 for information on instructional grouping of students within various content areas.)

d. *Alternate tasks.* If possible, the schedule should be designed so that highly preferred tasks alternate with less preferred tasks (the Premack Principle). For example, if most students don't like spelling, it could be scheduled right before P.E. because it is often highly preferred. In secondary schools, use this principle to plan activities within the class period. Some content areas are more highly preferred by teachers also. It is important that teachers do not spend excessive time on a particular area but learn to feel comfortable teaching all subjects or topics so that nothing is cut short.

2. *Manage noninstructional time.*

Organizational and transition times account for much of the noninstructional time during the day, including opening activities, lunch money collection, announcements, passing out materials, restroom breaks, clean-up time, and the like. Large amounts of time may be spent on organization and transition from one activity to another. As previously noted, teachers often do not realize how much time is actually

FIGURE 10–1 Sample Daily Class Schedule

8:15   Opening activities; homework check; special assignments

8:45   Individual assessment/instruction; independent work assigned on tasksheets

9:15   Reading block

Group A	Group B	Group C
9:15 Group with teacher activity (individual/group assessment instruction)	Independent work	Audiovisual or group
9:35 Independent work	Audiovisual or group activity	Group with teacher (individual/group assessment/instruction)
9:55 Audiovisual or group activity	Group with teacher (individual/group assessment/instruction	Independent work

10:15   Restroom break; recess or P.E., music, or art

10:45   Math block

Group A	Group B	Group C
10:45 Independent work	Group with teacher (individual/group assessment/instruction)	Self-correcting activity
11:00 Self-correcting activity	Independent work	Group with teacher (individual/group assessment/instruction)
11:15 Group with teacher (individual/group assessment/instruction)	Self-correcting activity	Independent work

11:30   Open time (individual conferences, storytime, timings, etc.

11:50   Lunch

12:15   Language arts (handwriting, spelling, composition)

1:00   Open time (individual conferences, timings, etc.)

1:15   Health, science, or social studies

1:45   Individual activities assigned on tasksheet; teacher conferences with individual students

2:15   Closing activities; dismissal

Source: Adapted from *Assessment for instruction* by S. S. Evans, W. H. Evans, & C. D. Mercer (1986). Boston: Allyn and Bacon. Copyright © 1986 by Allyn and Bacon. Reprinted by permission

spent in noninstructional activities until they analyze it in detail. For example, a 9:30 reading period may actually start at 9:40 every day after chairs are arranged in the reading circle and materials are passed out. A recurring 10-minute daily deviation becomes 50 minutes over the course of a week. When all the noninstructional time is totaled, it may amount to as much as 10% to 20% of the allotted time. It is crucial to teach students to eliminate nonessential activities and appropriately manage their noninstructional time, minimizing factors that compete with instruction. With practice, students may be taught how to perform organizational tasks and handle transitions efficiently and quickly.

3. *Develop guidelines for management of daily schedules.*
   The following suggestions may help in implementing the daily schedule:

   a. *Establish an opening routine.* Establish a routine to open each day (or class period in the case of secondary classes) so that students know exactly what to expect or do. Many teachers have an activity waiting for students on their desks or on the chalkboard so they don't wander aimlessly about the room. The activity should help begin the day/period on a positive note (solving a riddle, completing a puzzle, making a birthday card for a student, completing a holiday activity, writing in a journal, etc.). Meanwhile, the teacher may be checking homework or completing noninstructional tasks like lunch count. When everyone has arrived, begin the daily activities according to the schedule.

   b. *Post schedules.* Post a weekly schedule for the class and give each student a daily individualized schedule with time cues. Although routine is important, build variety into the schedule by occasionally changing the order of tasks or substituting a special activity for a regular one. Be sure to include plenty of active learning tasks. (A sample individual schedule is provided in Figure 10-2.)

   c. *Organize and prepare.* Make sure lesson plans and materials for the day are prepared and papers are graded before school begins. Instructional programs are likely to be less effective if they are haphazardly organized. Additionally, teachers expect students to be prepared, well organized, and careful in their work. The same should be expected of teachers. It is always important to remember that the teacher is a fundamental model for student behavior.

   d. *Seek assistance.* Enlist the help of others in planning and adhering to individual daily schedules. Encourage parents to get children to school on time. Stress the importance of the schedule to volunteers who are helping in the classroom. A timer may be used occasionally to help adhere to the schedule. To avoid unnecessary interruptions, try posting a sign with a note pad outside the classroom door that states: "Our time is very valuable. Please leave a note or see me after

FIGURE 10–2 Individual Schedule (adapted from class schedule)

8:15	Opening activities; homework check; special assignments
8:45	Individual math assignment (in folder)
9:15–10:15	Reading
9:15	Group A with teacher (reading table)
9:35	Independent work (assignment will be given out during group time)
9:55	Learning center (complete reading cooking activity with volunteer)
10:15	Restroom break; recess or P.E., music, or art
10:45–11:45	Math
10:45	Group B with teacher
11:00	Independent work (assignment will be given out during group time)
11:15	Math (activity on Mighty Math Machine [computer])
11:30	Book conference with teacher
11:50	Lunch
12:15	Language arts (discussion of report writing, spelling test with volunteer)
1:00	Practice timings
1:15	Continue social studies project
1:45	Individual activities assigned on tasksheet
2:15	Closing activities; dismissal

school. If you would like to come into our class, please check the list of things to do at the volunteer table."

4. *Increase engaged academic learning time.*

As noted in Chapter 6, time allocated to subject areas is important, but quality time and the time that students are actively engaged in a relevant task are more sensitive predictors of achievement and academic success.

a. *Actively involve students.* To ensure that students are motivated, attending, and engaged in learning, a variety of tasks that require active responding should be emphasized. A math skill may be strengthened, for example, by requiring the student to complete 10 problems rather than 1. The math problems, however, should require the student to respond in a variety of ways and be more than simply rote recitation. Problem solving and instructional activities that require students to apply and extend skills are useful in gaining interest. Teachers can do much to foster active learning by asking questions and encouraging students to fully and critically explain answers. Moreover, an effective teacher will give students frequent opportunities to respond actively during group instruction and individual activities. Materials and assignments should match student abilities and skills in all subject areas, not just reading or math.

b. *Guide students to assume responsibility.* Encourage students to take responsibility for planning and keeping to their individual schedules and knowing what to do when a particular assignment has been completed. Have motivating alternative assignments or activities ready for students who finish their work early, or allow them to work as volunteers helping other students. Remember to praise students who use their time efficiently and stay on-task. As students learn to take responsibility, teachers may allow more flexibility in the schedule and may make longer and more complex assignments.

c. *Schedule practice sessions.* Set aside time blocks each day to practice skills. "Timings" (short, timed samples of skills such as math facts, handwriting, or oral reading) can be used for proficiency practice in basic skills. Students can be taught to time themselves using a stopwatch and should be encouraged to compete against themselves, self-correct, and chart their progress. Additionally, peers may be paired to assist each other in timings, which are generally motivating, challenging, and fun.

5. *Cautiously plan pull-out instruction.*

Although pulling students out of a regular class for additional help or enrichment in another class may have a number of benefits, fragmented instruction may occur if the schedule is not carefully arranged. Occasionally, students are pulled out of the classroom too often and miss crucial content and continuity of an instructional program. As a result, some students may receive less instruction than they need in an important academic area. Moreover, students may receive conflicting instruction if methods, materials, or approaches of the special teacher are incompatible with those of the regular teacher. Teachers often find it difficult to keep track of who was out of class during which lesson. The irony is that schools are really attempting to provide these students with extra assistance.

6. *Judiciously schedule teacher paperwork.*

Beginning teachers are often simply overwhelmed by the mass of paperwork that confronts them. If paperwork is not handled efficiently, critical reports will not be submitted in a timely manner, instructional time will be compromised, and frustration will result.

a. *Learn to prioritize.* A critical first step is to prioritize paperwork. Not all paperwork is of equal importance. Some may be completed by teacher aides or volunteers. Other paperwork, however, is critical for legal or program reasons. These documents may be simply listed in a log as to the receipt and deadline dates and may be kept in an easily accessible area for teacher review.

b. *Develop a schedule for completing paperwork.* It may be helpful to devote a specific period of the day for completing paperwork. Thirty minutes at the beginning or end of the day is often sufficient for this purpose. Unfortunately, many teachers do not schedule time in this manner; what results is a mound of paperwork that requires hours to complete.

c. *Use technology to complete paperwork.* Computers may be used to generate educational plans; progress reports; letters to fellow teachers, parents, and students; and a host of other repetitive activities. Mimeograph and photocopying machines may also be used to reproduce documents such as class lists that are repeatedly requested. When technology is used in this manner, time is gained and instruction is enhanced.

d. *Use self-correcting materials.* Self-correcting materials assist in reducing the time that teachers must spend grading. Answer keys at a checking station, peer checking, and instructional materials with attached answers are but a few of the ways that self-correction can be used in the classroom.

Before using self-correction, students should be fully informed of their responsibilities and how self-correction will be used. Posting and reiterating rules as well as spot checking will eliminate much of the desire to cheat. When cheating does occur, the student should be counseled and allowed to use self-correcting procedures only after some assurance is provided that he or she will not cheat again.

Self-correcting procedures should not be used with all instructional activities or at all times. Moreover, students should be cycled out of materials that they have repeatedly self-corrected.

e. *Correct while circulating.* While moving through the class, check student papers quickly, thus providing immediate and corrective feedback and reducing the necessity for grading at a later time. Correct responses can be quickly noted and suggestions for improvement should be legibly written on the student's paper. When errors are noted, timely questions can be asked to determine the exact nature of the student's confusion. As a result, the feedback is both immediate and relevant.

CHAPTER 11
INSTRUCTIONAL GROUPING OF STUDENTS

DETECTION Watch for these problems:

- All of the low-ability students have been placed in one group for instruction.
- Students are not engaged in the assigned task.
- Instruction wanders and has little focus.
- Instructional groups function in turmoil.
- Students express confusion about the task assigned.

Grouping refers to how a class of students is organized to participate in instruction. Traditionally, an entire class was taught as a single unit, although working with subgroups was necessary in one-room schools where one teacher taught students of all ages and abilities. As educators learned more about individual differences, interests, and abilities, they began to diversify how they taught. In reading, for example, students would be divided into three or more ability groups, and the teacher would work with each in turn while the others did seatwork.

Teachers have experimented with many kinds of groups—ability, interest, learning rate, and intelligence—ending with five or six for reading, three or four for mathematics, and two or three for spelling. In actual practice, there is a point of diminishing returns related to the time, effort, management, and organization needed to make so many different groups function effectively in a classroom.

Instructional grouping is a critical instructional decision. While some tasks and skills can be taught individually, the reality is that much daily instruction is best conducted in a group setting. Inappropriate grouping of students or mismanaging groups leads to frustration for both teacher and student.

●●

An Instructional Problem

Jon Pavol really thought he was doing the right thing when he and Janice Lindzer divided their two classes of fifth-graders into ability groups for math instruction. Janice worked with the high- and medium-ability students, while Jon focused on the low-ability group. The concept seemed reasonable when they planned it. With Janice teaching all the faster students, Jon would have a smaller group and more time to work with individuals. Unexpectedly, however, the low group has developed a negative attitude about math, leading to discipline problems and lower achievement. Janice is content, since her groups are achieving and pleasant to instruct. Jon, however, is ready to insist they disband the math groups, even though Janice will oppose the idea.

●●●

CORRECTION Try these strategies:

1. *Establish ability groups.*

> *Ability grouping* (sometimes called *homogeneous grouping*) is an impre-cise term used to describe grouping students based on their past school performance. These groups can be large, medium, or small in size. Placing students of different ability levels into groups by random assignment or some other conscious design is *heterogeneous* grouping. Many schools have high-, medium-, and low-ability classrooms for stu-dents of the same age. Homogeneous grouping may also be used with de-partmentalized grade levels: One teacher may have all the slower students for reading instruction, another may work with the advanced group, while the third may instruct the average group.
>
> When high-achieving students work in the same group as low-achieving classmates, the low achievers tend to benefit most. When high-achieving students work in a group with high and low achievers, both benefit. But when low achievers work in a group without the assistance of more able students, their achievement suffers. Consequently, if low-ability students work only in low-ability groups, there are limited opportunities for peer assistance. This occurs most frequently in so-called tracked programs.
>
> Tracking is assumed to promote achievement by allowing the school to provide individualized instruction based on the perceived potential of each student. This assumption is not supported by reports in the pro-fessional literature. Students do indeed bring differences with them to school, but schools help widen these differences by ability grouping and providing knowledge, opportunities to learn, and classroom environ-ments vastly different for each group.
>
> Specific suggestions for effectively using ability groups include:
>
> a. *Use whole-class grouping (heterogeneous) for initial instruction.*
> b. *Use whole-class grouping (heterogeneous) for regular practice and skill reinforcement.*

c. *Use ability grouping (homogeneous) for corrective instruction or remediation.* The grouping should be temporary and last only until the students have achieved the purpose for which the group was formed.

d. *Use ability grouping (homogeneous) for enrichment activities following lecture, demonstration, or direct instruction.* The grouping should be temporary and last only until the students have achieved the purpose for which the group was formed.

e. *Use a combination of homogeneous and heterogeneous grouping.* For example, two days a week use ability groups for remediation or enrichment, and the other three days use whole-class instruction for group learning and practice activities.

●●●

An Instructional Problem

The students in the third-period gym class are bored. These seventh-graders are sitting in the bleachers of the gym, and a substitute teacher is talking about technique for running a zone defense. She has ignored attempts by the group to ask questions and has stubbornly continued to describe in detail major and minor tactics that can be used to attack the zone. The students become more restless as she continues. Finally one calls out, "Hey, lady, how about some time on the court?"

●●●

2. *Use lecture groups.*

The lecture group approach is a direct strategy for teaching in which the teacher tells the students what is to be learned, and the information is presented in its final form. Lecture groups are most often composed of all the students in the class or several classes combined. The teacher makes a formal presentation with a minimum of interaction by the students. The primary advantage of the lecture group is that large amounts of material can be delivered in a short period of time.

Most teachers can plan and deliver good lectures. To be effective, however, they must have a firm grasp of the content and organize it such that it will be intelligible and interesting to all students. Clarity is vital with this group strategy. If poorly planned or inappropriately used, the lecture group will lack stimulation and foster disruptive behavior.

The lecture group is both necessary and desirable for occasions at all grade levels. Because students are relegated to a passive role, the amount of student-teacher interaction needed for an evaluation and feedback is curtailed. In general, the lecture group is more appropriate for older students seeking large volumes of low-level cognitive information.

Specific suggestions for effectively using a lecture group include:

a. *Relate the presentation of new information to that which the students have already learned.* Review the connections between the two.
b. *Use an advance organizer.* Outline for the group the objectives for the lecture, the main points, and what they should concentrate upon.
c. *Begin the lecture with an attention grabber—an anecdote, a humorous bit of stagecraft, or a brief personal interaction.* Doing so will ensure that the group will begin the session engaged in the activity.
d. *Project confidence in one's understanding and mastery of the material.* The teacher's credibility and the group members' willingness to participate depends on establishing expertise.
e. *Present the content in a logical and ordered sequence.* A lecturer who makes unnecessary jumps forward and backward makes it difficult to understand what is being presented. Listeners are likely to become frustrated and annoyed.
f. *Use questions during the lecture to get feedback from the group.* Asking relevant questions will encourage the group to stay engaged in the task and identify concepts that need further explanation.
g. *Monitor nonverbal behavior to determine receptivity.* If several members of the group look puzzled or bored, stop and use questions to see what has not been understood and perhaps regain their attention.
h. *Use voice inflection, animated body movement, and gestures to emphasize key points.* Students are conditioned to respond to cues about what a speaker thinks is important. Holding up three fingers and saying "There are three things about this . . ." is a cue to the listeners that something important is about to be said. Without cues, the lecture group cannot determine what is really important.
i. *Be receptive to student questions during the lecture.* Questions from the group indicate what needs more discussion and what links to other material need to be made stronger.

●●

An Instructional Problem

Jake Bloom teaches chemistry at Forrest High School. As the new department chairperson, he must demonstrate a weekly experiment to the four honors chemistry classes in the school's teaching auditorium. Jake is by nature shy and thus uncomfortable being thrust in front of 73 students once a week. The students contribute to Jake's problems with an increasing stream of complaints: "We can't hear Mr. Bloom;" "He never relates what he is doing to what we are learning in class;" "I can't see what he is doing," and "We have to wait while he finds the equipment he needs," are the kinder comments from the students.

●●

3. *Arrange demonstration groups.* In the demonstration group the teacher shows what is to be learned. Demonstrations are most effective with moderate- to small-sized groups. If done properly, a demonstration can be like a picture—worth a thousand lecture groups. In the demonstration group students can watch and listen rather than just hear about something. It is an acceptable substitute for students doing an activity themselves. For example, in cases where direct student activity is too dangerous or time consuming, demonstration can be substituted.

The basic strength of an effective demonstration is the provision of a concrete example. Facts may be illustrated and verified and abstract concepts made more meaningful. The demonstration group also provides the opportunity for students to sharpen their observation, induction, and deduction skills. In some cases a well-organized demonstration is more effective in building concepts than if the students worked independently. All points considered, the demonstration group is very economical in terms of time, materials, and effort.

Specific suggestions for effectively using a demonstration group include:

a. *Carefully plan the demonstration.* Preparation should include practicing the demonstration to (1) determine if the procedure is going to provide the expected results, (2) identify the materials and tools needed, and (3) polish the narrative that will accompany the demonstration.

b. *Prepare a study guide for the students.* At minimum, students should answer a set of questions about what they experience during and after the demonstration. If the content is complex, a written narrative should be provided to help students understand the concepts presented.

c. *Make sure every student can clearly see and hear the demonstration.* This is not always easy. The further a student must sit from the demonstration, the greater the probability that he or she will not hear or see something. Equipment such as overhead projectors and sound amplifying systems is useful for demonstration groups exceeding 15 or 20 students. If the equipment and technical assistance is available, the demonstration can be videotaped. This allows students who missed the demonstration to see it and for group review of specific portions of the procedure. Videotaped demonstrations can also be collected and stored in a library for future use.

d. *Ensure the demonstration is relevant to the instruction ongoing in the classroom.* If the content is not correlated with daily student academic activity, students will perceive the demonstration to be a "show," diversion, or time filler.

e. *Begin the demonstration with a brief overview.* This is an advance organizer intended to focus the group's attention on the major concepts and procedures of the demonstration.

f. *Elicit participation by the students.* Ask the group to answer questions or physically participate in elements of the demonstration. This stimulates engaged time and provides a check for student understanding.
g. *Conclude with a short question and answer session.* This permits the group leader to summarize and clarify the main points of the demonstration. It also facilitates further understanding by the students.
h. *Provide an opportunity for immediate practice.* Students should complete the study guide or begin a follow-up learning activity as soon as the demonstration has ended.

●●●

An Instructional Problem

"What a waste," exclaimed Ms. Carnes as she swept into the teachers' lounge. "The kids were so indignant about the Supreme Court decision announced this morning that I let them discuss it in class instead of work on their civics reports. All they wanted to do was talk about how it would affect their friends or friends of friends or others who they knew might be a target of the ruling." Ms. Carnes sipped her coffee and continued, "I never heard such a mess of claptrap as they were spouting. I finally told Janet and Paco I didn't want to hear anymore of their whining. If they were going to participate, it would have to be on an objective level." Out of breath, Ms. Carnes sat and glowered.

●●

4. *Facilitate discussion groups.*

The most commonly used—and misused—group in secondary and elementary education is the discussion group. Teachers are most successful with students who are organized by interest and in small groups when using a discussion approach to instruction. It encourages positive thinking and attitudes, such as open-mindedness, flexibility, and objectivity. A discussion group can tie student interests and personal experiences to the subject for discussion, which increases the value of personal experience, enhances interest, and encourages participation. A further strength of the discussion group is that it can be used to develop higher orders of thought processes in students. When students are required to publicly present their ideas and feelings and receive feedback, it causes them to analyze their thinking. Teachers facilitate the discussion group by carefully planning their questions in order to move students to higher thinking levels. Discussion groups work best if the participants feel free to contribute and believe their comments are valued. Teachers must acknowledge the importance of competing views and ensure that all members of the group have an opportunity to be heard fairly.

Discussion groups are very time consuming. Teachers must decide if the time spent in discussion is worth the anticipated gains in student motivation and learning. In particular, teachers must consider that large chunks of material can be covered in lecture and demonstration groups faster than in discussion groups.

Specific suggestions for effectively using a discussion group include:

a. *Structure the discussion group.* Prepare objectives and organize the content to provide at least a framework for the discussion. Some discussion groups are effective if spontaneous, but most require planning and preparation.

b. *Provide background information and resources.* Students will bring only what they have experienced to the discussion group. It is the teacher's responsibility to augment this with additional information relevant to the topic.

c. *Use preplanned questions to guide the discussion.* Without some structure the discussion will lose focus and drift off to unrelated subjects.

d. *Encourage student-to-student interaction.* Structure the seating so members of the group can see each other without turning. Insist that students call each other by name and address comments to each other when appropriate.

e. *Accept student contributions as worthwhile.* Do not impose a value system that serves to eliminate other views and opinions from the discussion.

f. *Encourage the group to explore student contributions.* Do not let a divergent opinion or "pat" answer go unexamined. Expect and demand critical thinking from the group.

g. *Stimulate hesitant or unwilling students to participate in the discussion.* The group leader may have to call on individuals for contributions.

h. *Keep digression to a minimum.* Some digression is necessary, and some is very valuable to the overall goals of the discussion. In general, however, guide the group back to the topic as soon as possible.

i. *Interject short summaries throughout the discussion to maintain the focus.* Members of the discussion group get caught up in the process and sometimes lose sight of the goals.

●●

An Instructional Problem

Li Chin raised his hand, and Professor Wiles called on him. "Dr. Wiles," began Li, "something happened today that really upset me. Mr. Portello, my supervising teacher, had asked me to provide a 40-minute activity related to his science unit on plants and trees. I thought it would be a good idea to have the kids collect different kinds of leaves and make a notebook, so I put them into pairs and we walked over to Estis Park." Li paused and Dr. Wiles prodded, "Go on Li." "Well," he continued, "most of the kids picked up one or two leaves and then started to play. Before I could get them back to school, two kids had crossed the street and stolen some candy from the drug store, and the rest were throwing rocks at each other."

●●

5. *Implement learning activity groups.*

In learning activity groups, students manipulate objects or equipment under the direction of the teacher. Manipulation may involve students' use of concrete materials to solve a mathematical problems (e.g., counting or beads or forming sets of sticks). Learning to use equipment (e.g., typewriters and computers) is also accomplished via manipulation in learning activity groups. The group usually involves several small groups working to accomplish a specific task.

The typical learning activity group may serve to achieve one or more purposes:

- To secure new knowledge or develop new skills.
- To apply previously learned concepts to new situations.
- To reinforce previously learned information and practice previously learned skills.

A teacher must attend to a number of prerequisites to ensure that a learning activity group functions successfully. First, the activity selected must correlate with instructional goals and objectives. Second, sufficient background must be provided prior to implementing the group. Next, the roles and expectations must be delineated for the students. Fourth, appropriate study guides must be developed for use by the students.

Specific suggestions for effectively using learning activity groups include:

a. *Prepare the students for the activity group.* Tell them what the objectives are, what activities will be done, and how the material fits with what they have been studying.
b. *Put the students into groups of two or three.* Pair high- and low-ability students whenever possible.
c. *Provide ample time for the students to complete the assigned activities.*
d. *Have each group maintain a record of its activity and findings.*
e. *Conduct follow-up discussion after the activities have been completed.*
f. *Allot time for presenting reports and findings as necessary.*

•••

An Instructional Problem

"That's enough!" ordered Lou Kilpatrick. "I thought the class would enjoy playing this game, but I see you are not mature enough for it. For the past 15 minutes your comments to each other have gotten meaner and meaner, and now Linda is crying."

"Mr. Kilpatrick?" Erik was waving his hand to be recognized.

"What, Erik?"

"What were we supposed to be doing anyhow?" Erik asked, genuinely puzzled.

•••

6. *Plan instructional game groups.*

Instructional game groups are used with moderate- and small-sized numbers of students and may be classified into two major categories: simulation and nonsimulation. In simulation game groups students simulate authentic roles and experiences. By doing so, they become aware of a variety of situations before they encounter a real-life example. Many simulation games do not have winning as an objective; the activities are designed to simply provide vicarious experience. Nonsimulation games (e.g., vocabulary card games) do not involve role-playing as an integral part of the game.

Most instructional simulation games have three components—a player profile, a scenario, and rules for procedure. Active involvement of students is an advantage of using this type of group activity. Students realize that learning can be interesting and enjoyable. The instructional game group provides extensive opportunity for students to practice and improve their communication and decision-making skills.

A criticism of the instructional game group is that it mimics reality; real-life situations are not as simple as practiced in the game. This is particularly true when games are used to clarify controversial issues. Three additional criticisms are: (a) a lot of time may be required for both planning and implementing the group, (b) a limited number of students may participate in a group, and (c) it is difficult to monitor the progress of the group and the work of nonparticipating students.

Specific suggestions for effectively using instructional game groups include:

a. *Relate the instructional game group activity to ongoing classroom instruction.* Students must realize that the game group is a real part of their instructional program.

b. *Outline the game to the students before beginning.* Explain its purpose and the procedures to be used.

   c. *Firmly establish the rules of the game group.* Do so before the game begins, and enforce them strictly.

   d. *Provide direction during the game when needed.* Actively participate when possible, but do not control the student activity.

   e. *Provide an evaluation of the group's performance.*

●●

An Instructional Problem

Mr. Babbitt never reads the homework papers his students at Bayberry Boarding School turn in. He simply puts a checkmark on the paper and in his gradebook to note that it was received. He does the same thing for the tasks completed by his drill groups. He was astounded, however, when the entire entering class made exactly the same computational process error on the midyear math examination.

   "I swear, I don't know what is the matter with those kids," he told the headmaster. "I drill them on that specific skill at least once every marking period."

●●

7. *Use drill groups.*

   In the drill group students practice a skill after it has been acquired. Drill is necessary for students to obtain feedback about performing the skill. If done properly, drill has the important advantage of aiding retention and building mastery. If students understand a concept and are able to apply it in the drill group, the material will be remembered longer and more completely than if drill exercises are not used.

   Drill groups, like ability groups, are formed on the basis of past student performance and can be of moderate to small size. An important consideration in forming a drill group is the readiness level of the students. If the students lack the background to do the drills, the errors will likely be practiced and learned.

   Specific suggestions for effectively using drill groups include:

   a. *Make certain the students have an adequate understanding of the concept or skill before drill groups are used.*

   b. *Match the complexity of the drill activities with the individual attention spans and performance levels of the students.*

   c. *The teacher should circulate among the drill groups as they work to answer questions and give feedback.*

   d. *Make certain the students do not perceive drill group activities as punishment for their academic performance.*

   e. *The teacher must evaluate the result of drill-group work and give feedback to the students within one or two days.*

CHAPTER 12
EFFECTIVE USE OF MATERIALS AND EQUIPMENT

DETECTION   Watch for these problems:

- Teachers are sometimes unaware of certain materials available in the classroom.
- Guidance is needed to establish budgetary priorities.
- Some students appear to be victims of a flawed curriculum.
- Commercial materials are poorly-suited to most special-needs students
- Classroom learning does not always endure or necessarily find its way into normal daily usage.
- Few technological innovations are implemented.

More than a decade of litigation and legislation has sought to provide exceptional learners "equality of educational opportunity." It is estimated that 68% to 75% of all exceptional students receive a portion of their instruction in regular class settings. Unfortunately, figures suggest that only about one-third of these students are making satisfactory academic progress. Another 20% to 30% of the general student population evidence learning problems but lack the diagnostic labels required to be eligible for special education services.

The burgeoning number of students who fail to learn through traditional methods and materials offers strong testimony to the necessity for teachers to be knowledgeable about curricular analysis and adaptation. Studies suggest that a disproportionate amount of attention is often given to solving classroom deportment problems. Even so, quality instruction is a proven way of positively influencing student academic achievement and classroom conduct. This chapter examines ways to troubleshoot and make more effective use of materials and equipment in teaching regular and special-needs students.

Some authorities argue that too little emphasis is given to the curricular modifications needed to accommodate special-needs students.

The fact is, few classroom teachers have been prepared to deal successfully with the bewildering array of curricular decisions they face each day. In both special and regular classrooms, the learning problems of many students are exacerbated because few curricula have been field validated and thus proven effective before their introduction into the marketplace. Since students spend from 75% to 99% of their instructional time using commercial products, being able to detect and correct shortcomings of instructional materials is critical for special and regular classroom teachers alike. Since establishing so-called goodness-of-fit between student needs and curriculum is fundamental to quality instruction, strategies to improve the way in which materials are used in the classroom are discussed in this chapter.

CORRECTION   Try these strategies:

1. *Assess what is available.*
   To learn about curricular needs, first determine exactly what material—traditional and nontraditional—is available by conducting an inventory. Doing so will provide a basis for making later decisions about buying and/or adapting instruction materials. An inventory yields a clear picture of available materials, uncovers little used or forgotten materials, allows evaluation of the quality and usability of existing materials, and provides a purchase list that can be revised and updated as additional materials are acquired.

   a. *Categorize available materials.* A materials inventory may range from being simple to relatively complex. As illustrated in Figure 12–1, it usually consists of a list of available materials according to:
      1) name and publisher (e.g., Reading Mastery, SRA),
      2) description of the skills taught (e.g., synonyms, regrouping),
      3) quantity and teaching arrangements for which the material is best suited (e.g., small group or tutorial),
      4) material classification (i.e., core, drill and practice, or supplemental) and/or strategies for presenting the material (e.g., teacher demonstration),
      5) teacher analysis of its apparent usefulness (e.g., excellent—proven performance), and
      6) location in the classroom (e.g., back closet).
      Generally speaking, a materials inventory can be completed in as little as one to two afternoons. Once finished, it proves useful not only in reconsidering existing but also purchasing new instructional materials.
   b. *Specify skills to be taught.* Next, it is necessary to specify the skills students need to learn. Once individual academic needs (skills to be taught) have been determined, it is possible to organize old and obtain new materials to achieve these objectives.

FIGURE 12–1 Materials Inventory Form

Product	Publisher	Description	Quantity	Suitability	Classification	Analyzed Usefulness	Classroom Location

Additional Comments:

2. *Establish budgetary priorities.*

The commercial marketplace is flooded with attractive, seemingly appealing materials from which to choose. However, caution is necessary: While many of these materials look promising, their educational effectiveness may be questionable. With that caveat in mind, teachers must select wisely the type of instructional materials that are needed. Classroom materials can be grouped into several categories: core instructional materials, drill and practice materials, and free-time activities or enrichment materials. Generally, little money should be spent for diagnostic tests, drill and practice, or free-time materials. Curriculum-based tests, drill and practice, and free-time materials are the least expensive and simplest items for teachers to construct. Well-sequenced, validated core curricula (e.g., reading, spelling, arithmetic) usually should be the priority. Although a growing number of school systems provide materials for special as well as regular class instruction, some adaptation of these materials is usually required to accommodate special-needs students.

a. *Concentrate on core materials.* In establishing a new classroom program, funds should be expended on any core curricular items not available on a systemwide basis. Once core materials have been acquired, more latitude is possible in selecting supplemental materials. As a general rule, teachers should spend about 75% of available funds to establish or expand the core curriculum and 25% to obtain or maintain supplemental materials. It is also prudent to select materials that contain some content previously mastered. Many special-needs students are frustrated and often feel trapped in an educational system that is not in sync with their interests or abilities. Embedding old with new learning ("giving away success") can be a powerful teaching strategy.

b. *Supplement materials.* Once it has been determined that what is available falls short of standards, teachers must find ways to supplement instructional materials. Among potentially successful options are the following:

1) collaborate in the purchase of core materials with colleagues in the building (or possibly school system),

2) collaborate with colleagues in the construction and use of materials,

3) seek examination or sample materials from publishers,

4) obtain materials from companies on a try-out basis, and

5) use libraries to obtain materials on a short-term basis.

c. *Consider long-range needs.* It is essential to keep in mind long-range curriculum needs when constructing or purchasing materials. Any material that is 80% reusable is probably worth initial consideration from a cost-effectiveness standpoint. Some teachers estimate the worth of a material by calculating subjectively an efficiency-quotient. This formula takes into account the relative monetary expense, the time required for preparation in relationship to anticipated long-range instructional outcomes, and whether the time suggested by the publisher for routine classroom use (e.g., 20-minute lesson) fits into the existing schedule.

3. *Analyze instructional materials.*

Teaching materials—the so-called "tools of the trade"—must measure up to the rigorous demands of daily instruction. Teachers must be able to place students in proper curricular materials, detect instructional tactics that will enhance learning, maintain motivation, correct short-comings of materials, and monitor student performance in that subject area.

a. *Ask initial questions.* Experience suggests that initial questions regarding the instructional worth of materials are threefold:
   • Do the materials allow for proper evaluation and placement of students?
   • Are the materials and procedures necessary for monitoring student progress provided?
   • Is the instructional design of the materials such that the process of the curriculum and content of instruction are complementary?

   Clearly, it is wise to examine materials by asking these critical questions prior to purchase and classroom application.

b. *Identify placement procedures.* Few materials provide an assessment tool for curricular placement. For correct student placement, instructional materials that provide for curriculum-based assessment are the best choice. This is especially true if they contain behaviorally stated objectives that in turn are part of a well-organized sequence of instruction. Experience has proven that without quantifiable objectives, it is difficult to decide on the exact purpose of the materials, much less where to begin instruction. If it has been determined that placement procedures are completely lacking or inadequate, some kind of test will usually need to be constructed before the materials can be introduced into daily instruction. Ideally, the materials should allow students to begin receiving instruction at a variety of so-called entry points (i.e., each section of the instructional program should focus on specific subskills). Classroom instruction is often negatively influenced by deficits in student skills. It follows that prerequisite skills that correspond to each entry point should be stated in writing by the publisher (e.g., the specific reading level skills required in a general Earth Science series).

c. *Determine the content/instruction interface.* Materials analysis usually will reveal a lack of correspondence between curriculum and instruction. Determining the interface of content and instruction then becomes a critical aspect of the materials analysis.

Good curricular materials will include:

1) behaviorally stated objectives,
2) content that corresponds directly with those objectives,
3) content that is organized from simple to complex,
4) content that contains some redundancy, and
5) content that provides for teaching across stages of learning (i.e., from skill acquisition, proficiency building, to maintenance and generalization). A number of factors relate to the interface of curricular content and teaching methods. Namely, the materials should:
   - provide for ample practice of skills distributed across lessons
   - give students clear, understandable directions
   - prompt appropriate, frequent, and varied responses
   - provide sufficient clues and models for students that can be appropriately faded across time
   - offer immediate reinforcement for correct responses and remedial feedback for mistakes
   - adapt to various instructional arrangements (e.g., tutorial, independent or controlled seatwork, teacher-led instruction)
   - Emphasize maintaining and adapting knowledge/skills to new learning situations

d. *Locate or develop a measurement system.* Establishing an effective measurement system is closely aligned with curricular adaptation, since quality instruction depends on student assessment. Materials that do not allow for performance-based instructional decisions must be supplemented accordingly. Ideally, progress monitoring, mastery achievement, and maintenance and generalization measures should all be incorporated into the curriculum. Not surprisingly, few materials contain these measures. Then it becomes the teacher's responsibility to develop procedures for measuring these stages of teaching/learning.

Although few materials contain the means for detecting performance in these learning areas, there is growing recognition that the durability and generalizability of skills taught represent the ultimate criteria against which to judge an instructional material's worth. The problem of inadequate curriculum is sometimes compounded when teachers impose standards that are too low instead of establishing mastery criteria that would enable special students to compete with their regular classmates in integrated settings. Under most circumstances, mastery criteria should be established not only according to accuracy (i.e., percentage) but also rate of student performance (i.e., number of correct responses per minute). One way of correcting flawed materials and establishing meaningful criteria is to gather multiple work samples produced by successful students in regular classrooms and use it to calculate so-called peer-referenced standards. In carrying out daily instruction, the aim should be for students to approximate the accuracy and rate criteria of the "next-least restrictive environment" (e.g., a mainstream fifth-grade classroom).

●●●

An Instructional Problem

It just didn't seem fair. Bill and Manuel liked science very much. Unfortunately, both boys evidenced significant reading problems that limited their ability to complete the reading assignments. Mr. Kennedy thought about curricular adaptations that might accommodate the boys' special instructional needs but wasn't sure where to begin.

●●●

4. *Take corrective steps to improve instructional materials.*
     Oftentimes, it is clear that one or more aspects of the curriculum will have to be corrected prior to its introduction into classroom instruction. Whether materials are corrected in advance or following a try-out phase, several principles have proven useful to teachers.

   a. *Changes in materials usually will correspond to both the content and the measurement system.* Clearly, if the content is not appropriate, it will need to be corrected to accommodate individual objectives. By comparison, if the content is acceptable, the measurement system may still need to be examined (and perhaps modified) prior to using the materials. Content and measurement must be tied to the instructional objectives as well as the presentation strategies selected.
   b. *Few materials are well-suited to specialized instruction and will require some adaptation.* Once a measurement system is in place, the two remaining aspects of any materials that may need correction are curriculum content and teacher presentation. Figure 12–2 illustrates one approach to examining materials to detect possible curricular shortcomings.
     When critically examining materials, it is useful to record comments in the right column of the form, which contains a checklist of common corrections for each component of the curriculum. A checkmark indicates that changes are called for in a specific area. For instance, do objectives need to be written or simply revised? Is the content consistent with previously specified objectives? Are new skills or steps needed, or do existing skills/steps need correction or expansion? Similarly, the appropriateness of the teaching format

FIGURE 12–2 Curricular Analysis and Adaptation Form

Material Publisher and Description _____

_____

AREA	IDENTIFICATION PROBLEM	CHECKLIST
Curriculum	_____	Write objectives _____
Objectives	_____	Revise objectives _____
	_____	Use available list of objectives
		_____
		Other _____
		_____
Content		
Acquisition	_____	Add new content steps _____
Proficiency	_____	Add more response items_____
Maintenance	_____	Revise/Correct content steps _____
	_____	_____
Generalization	_____	New presentation format_____
	_____	Response mode_____
		Revise format_____
		Response mode_____
		Other _____
		_____
Sequence		
Critical elements	_____	Develop alternative sequence(s)
	_____	_____
Presentation order	_____	
	_____	
	_____	Develop steps/contents_____

FIGURE 12–2 Curricular Analysis and Adaptation Form (continued)

AREA	IDENTIFICATION PROBLEM	CHECKLIST

Sequence (continued)

*Redundancies*_____   Drop steps _____

_____   Add substeps_____

_____   Other_____

Measurement

Initial Detection_____   Revise test(s)_____

• *Placement* _____   Adapt test_____

• *Pre-Posttest*_____   Devise test_____

_____

Progress Monitoring_____   Revise probes_____

• *Daily/Weekly*_____   Devise probes_____

• *Self-checks* _____

Mastery Criteria_____   Detect accuracy_____

_____   Detect fluency_____

_____   Specify aim (dates)_____

_____   Specify trials_____

_____   Specify peer standards_____

_____   _____

_____   _____

Visual Display _____   Revise charts/graphs_____

_____   Add charts/graphs_____

_____   Group display_____

_____   Individual display_____

Maintenance and
Generalization _____   Specify aim date(s)_____

FIGURE 12–2 Curricular Analysis and Adaptation Form (continued)

AREA	IDENTIFICATION PROBLEM	CHECKLIST

Maintenance and Generalization (continued)

_____   Specify probe date(s)_____

_____   Specify new stimuli (e.g., settings, people, materials)_____

Instruction

Practice   _____

•*Massed*   _____   Slice/segment activities_____

•*Distributed*   _____   Add distributed practice_____

•*Controlled*   _____   Expand practice activity_____

Other_____

_____

Instructions/Directions_____   Write/simplify directions_____

_____   Vary directions_____

_____   Add advanced organizers_____

_____   Add directions in other modalities____

Other_____

_____

Student Response_____   Adapt response mode_____

_____   Remediate response mode_____

_____   Teach prerequisites_____

Other_____

_____

Prompts and Models_____   Revise/add prompt(s)_____
Revise/add demonstrations and permanent models_____

_____   Add physical guidance_____

_____   Other modality_____

_____   Other_____

_____

FIGURE 12–2 Curricular Analysis and Adaptation Form (continued)

AREA	IDENTIFICATION PROBLEM	CHECKLIST
Reinforcement	_____	Add external reinforcement (e.g., points, edibles, tokens) _____
Correction	_____	Add self-correction materials_____
	_____	Add self-monitoring materials_____
	_____	Provide additional practice materials, teacher-directed activity _____
	_____	Adjust pace _____
	_____	Other_____
	_____	_____
Teaching Arrangements_____		Revise teaching acts_____
	_____	Add 1:1 tutorial, group-individualized, or small-group format_____
Generalization	_____	Revise program_____
Training	_____	Add program_____

Additional Comments:

must be considered—arrangement for presenting the materials, as well as the anticipated student response to the materials (e.g., written or oral). Finally, the content sequence may be judged as adequate or in need of correction. Comparable decisions can be made on all aspects of curriculum (see Figure 12-2). If many areas appear to be especially deficient (i.e., evaluation yields numerous checkmarks), it may be wise to seek other materials better suited to the particular objectives identified for the students.

c. *Modify written and verbal directions.* Because some students have difficulty with written and verbal directions, those that accompany materials may need to be modified. Usually, correction can be accomplished by shortening sentence length/complexity or emphasizing key words (e.g., underlining). In other cases, it may be necessary to offer an explanation of terms that are ambiguous to the student. Additional directions for clarification may be presented via an audiotape to accompany written instructions.

Some students may be asked to respond in writing to instruction; others may be called upon for oral recitation. Pretaped instructions that contain several examples and nonexamples can be prepared so that students can review information repeatedly at their own pace. Decisions about adapting the student response should be linked to knowledge of their abilities and the real-life application of the skills taught. Most commercial materials rely on visual presentation of content and are designed to evoke a limited range of student responses (e.g., verbal or written). A common adaptation proven effective is to introduce highlight cues (e.g., color and/or size) to draw the student's attention to the relevant dimensions of an academic task. For example, underline key words or color-code related skills (e.g., application of letter-sound relationships). Written examples placed in close proximity to a student's work have also been found to be useful in spelling, arithmetic, and handwriting.

d. *Use contingencies.* The importance of the systematic application of classroom contingencies of reinforcement aimed at improving student performance is well established. However, few materials build in reinforcement strategies that are known to have instructional value. Introduction of immediate teacher feedback has usually proven effective. Teacher-led discussion of the specific relevancy of various subjects and lessons (i.e., extrinsic justification of instruction) often increases student interest and may reinforce student efforts. Beyond introducing effective teacher reinforcement, it is often necessary for the teacher to develop a reinforcement menu (e.g., a selection of available reinforcers) to promote student achievement through the use of individually tailored contracts. As suggested, previously learned skills should be routinely reintroduced, not only to bolster student confidence by maintaining a high rate of task success but also to serve as a teacher measure of retention.

FIGURE 12–3 Possible Areas of Misfit

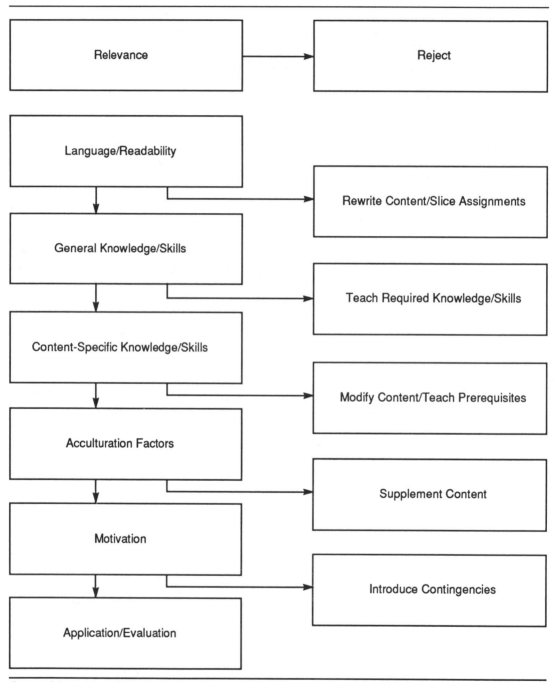

Source: Adapted from Gable, R. A., Hendrickson, J. M., & Young, C. C. (1987). A model for making instructional decisions for behavior disordered adolescents. In R. Rutherford, S. Forness, & C. M. Nelson (Eds.), *Severe behavior disorders of children and youth.* San Diego, CA: College-Hill. Reprinted by permission.

e. *Allow for overlearning.* Materials that allow for too little practice may impede student progress. The amount of practice, or redundancy, built into instructional materials, must be evaluated in relation to the objectives of instruction for each student. Sometimes, content may need to be "sliced" into smaller units and thus expanded for more learning opportunities.

   Even after practice with selected materials, some students may need sustained teacher guidance and feedback. Successful means of assistance include cues in the form of verbal directions, partial answers, or actual physical guidance.

f. *Fade corrective procedures.* Keep in mind that once students acquire a particular skill, some correction procedure will need to be systematically faded. For instance, teacher feedback on arithmetic computation during the beginning stages of instruction can be replaced with occasional "review frames" recorded on student worksheets. Also, special prerecorded audiotapes that contain information on instruction allow students to self-correct skill deficiencies. Figure 12-3 summarizes some of the areas in which a misfit may exist between curriculum and student, offering a corresponding corrective strategy, as well.

5. *Promote durable instruction.*

   In the final analysis, a student's ability to apply newly acquired skills in real-life situations represents the basis for judging the worth of instruction. It follows that programming to generalize academic gains is an important aspect of classroom instruction. As most experienced teachers will attest, few instructional materials contain a generalization component. Consequently, this shortcoming must be corrected to ensure that the critical issue of generalization is addressed.

   a. *Transfer generalization across settings, conditions and persons.* Only following repeated generalization training sessions is it reasonably certain that a student's response repertoire is large and flexible enough to endure and be appropriate across various settings, conditions, and persons. Training should emphasize the use of academic skills under conditions that vary from those encountered during the initial stages of instruction. Often, the materials themselves must be corrected, the type and schedule of student reinforcement adjusted (e.g., from frequent to occasional), and the setting in which a skill is performed varied (e.g., an arithmetic skill is applied under new conditions). Further, the students may need to be taught to modify the response itself according to the situation. That is, differing responses may need to be taught for varying occasions. Classmates may be called on to respond individually to materials of varying complexity or to answer questions posed. In this way, students are exposed to repeated and differing responses and are better able to generalize learning.

b. *Teach problem solving and increase difficulty.* Generalization training can be accomplished by introducing several other techniques. For example, promoting students' correct responses to questions on materials that contain extraneous or distracting matter (e.g., irrelevant information embedded in a reading problem) is a well-known strategy. To apply previously learned skills to new situations, training can be initiated so that problem-solving strategies (e.g., component analysis of problem resolution, covert verbal rehearsal) can be practiced by the student under conditions that compare to real life. Repeatedly assessing student performance will enhance determination of when it is appropriate to graduate to more demanding instructional material and which students need repeated training. Programming for generalization of academic skills should gradually but systematically move toward more functional and complex applications of the skills being taught (e.g., skills applied under natural conditions).

6. *Make use of technological innovations.*

The technological explosion in public education has produced a number of casualties, namely, students and teachers who have been left behind by significant advances. There are several simple ways of correcting this situation. For example, the use of audiotutorial programming is one way of incorporating available technology into classroom assessment and instruction. Audiotutorial instruction refers to the use of audio equipment in teaching. Usually, the teacher prepares academic material and then administers selected aspects of instruction by means of an audiotape (or videotape) recorder.

a. *Use audiotutorial programming.* Audiotutorial programming offers a means for individualizing instruction, provides a bridge between regular group and remedial one-to-one instruction, and allows for independent teaching of students, which offsets the sometimes negative aspects of adult-controlled instruction. An additional quality that underscores the value of audiotutorial programming is the opportunity it affords to include corrective instruction. Teachers can easily adapt a pretaped program so that a momentary pause for the student to respond is followed by the correct answer. A program can provide the student corrective feedback on responses at selected intervals (e.g., "If you answered question number 7, yes . . . "). For students to function independent of teacher control, it is advantageous to incorporate frequent self-checks during the initial stages of programmed instruction. These self-checks might consist of paper-

and-pencil exercises that accompany a taped program and call on the student to answer several short questions. Further, to increase the likelihood of success, a series of supervised practice exercises may be needed in which students are led step by step through a sample program (e.g., "free dictation" format for spelling). During this training phase, students should be taught how to operate the tape recorder or other equipment, plus how and when to respond. Here are five steps toward developing a tutorial program:

- Establish educational objectives in relation to student ability and instructional needs previously detected.
- Prepare instructional packets and materials (e.g., content to be learned and answer sheets) based on student abilities and needs in selected content areas.
- Develop administration procedures, either written or taped, that include instructions for student use of answer sheets, record forms, and so on.
- Place students in the program according to information obtained from cumulative folders or classroom data (e.g., curriculum-based tests).
- Introduce the program, observe, and evaluate student performance for purposes of making any necessary program corrections.

Equipment for conducting a tutorial program includes prerecorded tapes (e.g., math facts, spelling words, science lesson), a cassette audiotape recorder or VCR, and headphones.

b. *Use computer applications.* Computer-assisted instruction represents another major technological resource available to teachers. As with tutorial programming, computer-assisted instruction allows for promoting quality student performance without detracting from group instruction. Simple-to-operate software programs that may also include a voice synthesizer (e.g., for dictating spelling words in list or paragraph form) can save the teacher time, reduce mistakes in repeating instruction, and produce timely information for making instructional decisions. Selection of computer courseware is predicated on several factors, namely, accuracy of content, clarity of directions, motivational appeal, ease of student use, and correspondence with conventional classroom materials.

The future promises to bring a range of technological innovations for remedial and individualized instruction. In most instances, specialized training is necessary not only for the teacher but also for the student. Further, the daily instruction schedule along with the physical classroom organization may be affected to the extent that additional adjustments are needed.

c. *Promote the use of learning centers.* A learning center may be one solution that works well in curricular areas where skills are presented sequentially. Consider designating one area within the classroom for carrying out this form of instruction. A learning center can be organized around specific curricular areas (e.g., the Spelling Center, Math Center, or Science Center). It allows individualization of instruction according to more conventional paper-and-pencil materials, an audiotaped program, or computer-assisted instructional program.

Because mutual use of centers by students sometimes leads to disruptive social exchanges, prepare individual learner contracts linked to specific assignments to be completed at the center. Since sophisticated electronic equipment will accompany many of the instructional programs placed in these centers, introduce specific rules for and control practice of proper equipment usage before allowing students to work independently.

7. *Carefully adapt the curriculum to individual student needs.*

For most students, the decision for placement outside the regular classroom rests with persons recommending such options. Consequently, increasing numbers of special-needs students are being taught in mainstream classrooms. While knowledge of what represents an appropriate curriculum remains somewhat limited, the main goal is individualized instruction. Too often this goal has been synonymous with independent student seatwork (e.g., skill sheets, puzzles, flashcard drill). Perhaps as never before, the relationship has been recognized among learner needs and abilities, teaching strategies, and curricular content. It is mandatory that teachers possess the skills with which to detect and correct faulty instructional materials. Without curricular adaptation, individualized instruction is likely to remain more a promise than a reality for an increasingly diverse population of school-aged students.

In closing, consider the following guidelines:

- Instruct students in a systematic fashion, minimizing change for change's sake.
- Give every student ample opportunity to respond, correcting the frequency and complexity of responses on a student-by-student basis.

- Reinforce correct responses enthusiastically and provide immediate and appropriate feedback on errors.
- Limit the number of concepts introduced—emphasize depth over breadth.
- Allow for academic success by combining old with new materials and instruction.
- Incorporate redundancy into the curriculum.
- Avoid a "teach-and-hope" approach; plan for generalizing every important concept.
- Be patient and accept reward for good teaching.

CHAPTER 13
EFFECTIVE DELIVERY OF THE INSTRUCTIONAL PROGRAM

DETECTION   Watch for these problems:

- All students are expected to progress through the curriculum at the same rate.
- Students are advanced from one skill to the next regardless of skill proficiency.
- Skills that students learn are not maintained, generalized, or applied over time.

The traditional model of classroom teaching usually includes grade-level sequencing and dividing subject-area instruction into units or lessons with group pacing, whole-class instruction, and independent seatwork. Students are expected to progress through the curriculum at basically the same rate as age peers with the same amount of instruction and practice.

This model has persisted in public school teaching over the years and may be appropriate for the average students in the classroom. However, for students with learning/behavior problems, this lockstep approach may not meet their individual needs. Not all students learn at the same rate or come into the curriculum with the same set of readiness or prerequisite skills. Moreover, the learning and behavior problems that eventually occur may be partially due to the lockstep curriculum imposed on these students. As the curriculum becomes more difficult, some students are unable to master new skills and maintain the learning pace. However, due to the nature of the approach, they are advanced to the next task or next grade but possess a fragmented set of skills. Other students may be advanced too slowly through the curriculum and become bored and uninterested in the instructional program. With both kinds of students and approaches (underteaching and overteaching), the amount of task completion and on-task behavior decreases. These students become curriculum casualties, which eventually leads to learning and behavior problems.

●●●

An Instructional Problem

This was Ms. Fry's first year as a teacher. Her third-grade classroom curriculum was carefully planned well in advance. All subjects to be taught were neatly organized into units spaced evenly throughout the year. Students were divided into three groups for reading, but in other subjects, such as math, language arts, spelling, science, and social studies, whole-class instruction was used with group pacing and the same independent seatwork activities for everyone. All students were expected to progress through the curriculum at basically the same rate.

For 18 of her 25 students, the year went reasonably well. However, five of Ms. Fry's students had great difficulty keeping up with math. They were unable to master the new skills being taught because they didn't understand the prerequisite math skills; they just fell further and further behind. In spelling class, three children failed the spelling posttest week after week but on Monday were routinely presented with new spelling lists to learn. Three students that were placed in the lowest reading group were struggling to keep up. In all of the cases, due to the nature of the system, students were advanced to the next assignment or unit but with a fragmented set of skills and an increasing sense of frustration with school.

●●●

CORRECTION   Try these strategies:

1. *Accommodate stages of learning to meet individual needs.*

All students can master the curriculum if they are given enough time and the appropriate strategies are used. Teachers must vary learning times for individual students to allow mastery and proficiency of basic skills. There are several phases in the process of developing any given skill, falling in a hierarchy from initial exposure and gradual acquisition to proficient, fluent, and adapted performance. The six stages include acquisition, fluency, proficiency, maintenance, generalization, and application/adaptation.

- *Acquisition.* In the acquisition phase, the skill or behavior is first introduced. There may be a high number of incorrect or inappropriate responses and a low number of correct or appropriate responses. Often percentage measures are used to show accuracy of performance. Instruction at this stage is designed to improve skill accuracy. Therefore, accuracy of appropriate responses should increase while incorrect or inappropriate responses should decrease or be eliminated.

- *Fluency.* During the fluency stage, rate becomes an important issue. Accuracy has improved, and now the emphasis is on increasing the rate, frequency, or speed of the appropriate response. Skill practice is needed at this stage. Rate, or responses per minute, allows discrimination between students who are highly accurate but slow and students who are accurate but also fluent. Rate is a sensitive measure of performance and may be used to measure fluency and accuracy of response. Many of the important prerequisite skills that students continually use in school (such as writing answers to basic math facts and reading high-frequency sight words) must be performed at high rates to enhance success with more difficult tasks in the curriculum.
- *Proficiency.* At this stage, the skill is accurately and comfortably used at a high rate of speed. Practice continues. Performance on more difficult skills is enhanced if response rates of correct or appropriate behaviors approximate proficiency rates. Various methods may be used to determine proficiency rates, including normative data, performance rates of peers who are progressing acceptably, teacher judgment, or a student's previous performance. No matter what method is chosen, it is important that goals be adjusted to meet the unique needs of each learner.
- *Maintenance.* This stage involves a process to ensure that behavior improvements will persist under natural environmental conditions after formal programming and reinforcement are no longer provided. The desired skill or behavior must be at an acceptable level and maintained at this proficient level before withdrawing the teaching procedure or intervention. Maintenance does not usually occur automatically, which leads many teachers to assume that the teaching procedure or intervention used was faulty. If a skill or behavior is not used regularly, the teacher must review or require its use periodically to ensure it is being maintained.
- *Generalization.* This stage refers to behavioral changes that occur in conditions other than the original training conditions. *Generalization* is defined as the occurrence of a skill or behavior in response to new conditions—in another setting, with other individuals, or at another time. For example, if the behavior of saying "thank you" has been taught in the classroom, it is desirable that this behavior be generalized and exhibited in other settings with other people. At this stage, continued practice under a wide variety of conditions is important. It is also helpful to target skills or behaviors that will likely be reinforced by the natural environment.
- *Application/Adaptation.* The highest level in the hierarchy of learning stages, application/adaptation, involves using skills in modified form in response to new problems or situations without need for direction. Teachers cannot teach students specific behaviors for every condition they are likely to meet. If they are unable

to apply and adapt, students have limited control over their environment. These skills are important for predicting and reasoning, as well as divergent and creative thinking. Application/ adaptation is achieved by providing opportunities to meet as many new situations as possible, discriminating key elements, and formulating an appropriate response.

●●

An Instructional Problem

Mr. Stephens introduced a small group of students to the math skill of adding two digits to one digit with carrying. He modeled the skill on the blackboard, set performance goals for each student, and gave a short assignment. After completing the first few problems using this skill, Mr. Stephens provided immediate feedback to the students and asked them to rework the problems they had missed. During the next several days, the students had many opportunities to work on problems of this kind, increasing accuracy and then building rate and always receiving immediate feedback either from Mr. Stephens or an answer sheet at the self-correction station. In a short period of time, all of the students achieved proficiency in this skill. Because of the systematic and structured method of instruction, all of the students adapted this skill quickly to learn the more difficult skills of adding two digit plus two digit with carrying and three digit plus three digit with carrying, reaching proficiency even more quickly with these skills.

●●

2. *Individualize programming using the direct instruction model.*
Once a student has been appropriately placed in a curriculum and/or in an ability group, such as a reading group, the direct instruction model offers an effective and highly organized approach to individualizing instruction. Direct instruction includes the following characteristics:
- teaching the exact behavior of concern
- sequenced and systematic instruction and well-organized assignments
- setting clear and precise performance goals
- frequent and direct feedback to students about performance
- arranging consequences for appropriate or inappropriate performance
- active and frequent responding
- practice until mastery

Direct instruction does not mean repetitious, rote, meaningless, isolated learning. Rather, it is a well-organized approach that leads students through an effective process that helps them learn to learn and master simple skills, complex skills, and independent study skills. To use direct instruction in the classroom, the following steps should be followed:

a. *Determine the skills to be taught, and establish precise performance goals.* Carefully choose a sequence of skills based on specific, relevant, and individualized assessment, and then set short- and long-range objectives.

b. *Prepare the student for instruction by using advance organizers.* Outlining a content area, discussing relevant vocabulary, or providing background information about a particular skill or concept helps set the stage for instruction. It also may help determine what prior knowledge individual students bring to a discussion or unit of study, thereby enabling more individualization.

c. *Model or demonstrate the skill.* Most students learn better if they can see a skill performed and then imitate the steps. Each step should be demonstrated while being described aloud by the teacher so the students can see all the processes involved. The students may then model the skill while repeating the steps verbally as the teacher demonstrates again.

d. *Provide controlled practice and feedback.* Students should have many opportunities to practice the skill while receiving individual, frequent, specific, and corrective feedback about performance. Continued practice will lead to improved accuracy and fluency.

e. *Encourage generalization.* Generalization is often a neglected aspect of the teaching process. However, it is crucial that skills are generalized to real, meaningful situations and maintained over time. Students should be given tasks requiring skill application in a variety of situations (such as using specific measurement skills learned in math for an art project).

3. *Ensure educational success.*

If students are appropriately placed in the curriculum, individual learning rates and styles are considered, and a direct instruction model is used, there is a better chance of academic success. Additionally, several other teacher- and student-related variables are significantly related to the effective delivery of the instructional program.

a. *Vary activities.* The teacher should vary the types of instructional activities (whole-class instruction, small-group instruction, individual instruction, seatwork activities, peer tutoring, cooperative learning) used through the day and the year. It is important to achieve a good balance and meet the needs of all students.

b. *Differentiate instruction.* Within-class ability grouping should still offer differentiated instruction and assignments for individual students within the group. Students that may have trouble keeping up with the group should be provided with more individualized instruction. Peer tutoring or cooperative learning may be a way to accomplish this.

c. *Expect the best.* Teachers should set and communicate high expectations concerning academic and social behavior. Teacher expectations about certain students based on a label, past records, or another teacher's report may alert teachers to potential problems and may cause them to treat these students differently. Such expectations may ultimately lead to a self-fulfilling prophecy: Students tend to learn as much or as little as their teachers expect. Low expectations may be unknowingly communicated to a student, leading to decreased motivation and poor performance when he or she might have succeeded under different expectations.

d. *Remember, the student knows best.* The level of achievement and unique needs of each student should guide instruction. Teachers should be willing to change course whenever necessary to meet the changing needs of each student. Because so many variables in the student's environment have an impact on learning, the teacher should be alert to those factors that influence learning in each subject area and alter the program as needed to keep it relevant, appropriate, and motivating.

4. *Continuously evaluate students in a timely and positive manner.*

Students, regardless of age, are constantly changing and learning. As a result, there is a constant possibility of problems. If students are haphazardly or infrequently evaluated, it is likely that instructional problems will go undetected and grow in magnitude and severity. For this reason, student work should be graded and constructive feedback provided as immediately as possible.

a. *Understand the function of grades.* Certainly, grades are used to differentiate and evaluate the accuracy and thoroughness of student responses. Little is accomplished, however, by simply recording the repeated failures of students. A constant stream of failing grades on instructional activities should sound a warning bell. It is clearly inappropriate to simply continue giving failing grades without attempting to discern the fundamental cause for failure. This pattern of failure creates a negative expectation on the part of the teacher and, more importantly, eliminates student desire to learn or participate.

b. *Accentuate the positive.* Note correct responses and strengths in answers to foster student participation. Suggestions for improvement can be given kindly and sandwiched between positive comments. A student, for example, who fails to adequately explain the main idea of a story may be told that he or she has correctly identified many of the details while at the same time questioned and encouraged to do more. Contrast this positive method of evaluation with the negative practice of simply noting that the answer was incomplete and unacceptable.

Teachers must never forget to treat students with the same care, dignity, and kindness that they wish to be treated with. This is not to say that evaluation cannot be critical. Rather, it illustrates that people of all ages work harder and better and enjoy activities more when the positive is accentuated.

CHAPTER 14
EARNING THE JOY AND
SATISFACTION OF TEACHING

This chapter deviates from the Detecting and Correcting format to offer a closing narrative. In short, facets of education profession impinge upon one's ability to successfully perform in the classroom. Considering a few of these may put the teaching role into a more understandable perspective.

When salespeople talk about what keeps them in the business, it is not the the commission, company car, or free trips. It is the internal pleasure that comes from successfully "teaching" a customer the advantages and benefits of purchasing a specific product.

A teacher's motivation for returning to the classroom day after day is also internal. Few things compare with the joy and satisfaction evoked when a child grasps a new idea and, bristling with eagerness, demands "Let's do it again!"

Teaching, like selling, is not easy to master. At best, a teacher-training program prepares an individual with entry-level skills. Following this training, one must work diligently to acquire the tools to be successful. The first year in the classroom is marked by long hours of preparing lessons, constructing materials, and experimenting techniques. Each succeeding year it is easier to plan and manage, as experience and practice sharpen skills and judgment. In general, an individual must "pay dues" for three to five years before earning the title of *teacher*.

Successful teachers accept three important conditions of their profession. First, they learn schooling's equivalent of laboratory versus field research. In the laboratory, for example, a scientist can control every aspect of an experiment so that relationships between variables can be precisely identified and described. Extending the results of laboratory findings to natural settings, however, is more difficult because the experimenter cannot completely control an application. The resulting evidence for establishing relationships between variables is imprecise and clouded with alternative explanations. Teachers are bombarded with pronouncements and nostrums from clinical experiments and school reformers guaranteed to improve the rate and quality of classroom learning. In the application, however, teachers apply and shape the techniques as necessary to make them effective with little regard for theory. The first rule of applying an innovation is: Make it work or discard it.

Second, children are not raw materials to be shaped into products meeting an industry standard. The president of a *Fortune* 500 company is entitled to believe that schools are not doing an adequate job of educating children. Adapting the business procedures of his or her firm for solutions, however, is arguable. For example, when he or she asserts vendors are required to submit raw materials to the production plants that meet exact specifications and that the company will not ship a flawed product, he or she exhibits ignorance of uncontrolled social, political, and school conditions that directly affect a teacher's ability to educate a child. Teachers have no influence over a child's genetic heritage or the environmental experiences of a child's first five or six years of life. In essence, schools have no quality control of raw materials and must accept whatever "the vendors" submit.

When the school does assume responsibility for educating a child, it controls only about 12% of the time available during the 12 or 13 years in which public schooling occurs. In addition, 20 or more different people will work with the child. Most will not know the others, all will have varying abilities and skills, and each will have a different idea of what is important for the child to learn. Teachers must understand and accept children as diverse individuals with unique strengths and weaknesses. A manufacturing model for educating human beings is neither possible nor practical.

Third, learning is marked by frequent processing pauses. Education reformers and critics ignore this fact. They state or imply that every moment of a child's classroom time can be filled with excitement and learning. Practicing teachers know that the classroom routine is more akin to pitching a baseball game. Batters safely hit a pitched ball, on average, two to three times for every ten times at bat. But a pitcher will throw six, seven, or more times to each batter. Consequently, a baseball game consists of constant activity by the pitcher and catcher, while seven other players stand about waiting for the batter to hit the ball. Of course, when a ball is hit, a flurry of activity is followed by a return to waiting.

A teacher is always "pitching" material to the students and waiting for the learning to "hit." It takes repeated pitches for a student to process material. Teachers revel in the moment a student or class fully grasps a concept because it is followed by the next round of presenting and practicing while processing takes place.

TEACHER ATTRIBUTES

A teacher is more likely to consistently obtain satisfaction from teaching if he or she possesses or works to acquire five basic attributes: senses of humor, perspective, problem solving, personal involvement, and self-worth.

Sense of Humor

Next to intelligence, a sense of humor may be the most useful attribute a person can possess. It can be armor against daily stress, a tool for resolving interpersonal conflict, or medication for curing emotional hurts. A teacher's ability to laugh at the antics of first-graders on a cold, rainy Monday is the difference between finishing the day upbeat or with angry, sullen children. The skill to use gentle humor to point out the absurdity of a seventh-grader's demand for special privileges resolves the tension and avoids a confrontation. Sharing with a close colleague 10 ways to terminate an insensitive and bullying administrator helps soothe the hurt of being demeaned in a faculty meeting.

Sense of Perspective

A teacher's ability to keep the demands of teaching in perspective is critical to making sound judgments and maintaining personal harmony. Having a sense of perspective means knowing the appropriate relation of the parts to the whole. Too often teachers are so involved in the details of managing a classroom and the individual needs of children that they lose sight of how everything is related. Their viewpoint narrows until the details become the whole and the "big picture" is lost.

Perspective also means determining the relative importance of events from a specific point of view. Many teachers are concerned with the right or wrongness of what they do in the classroom. But actually, there are few absolute rights or wrongs in teaching. Rather, presentations, actions, and reactions are effective, neutral, or ineffective. Removing the value judgment from one's perspective and focusing on the quality and quantity of results produces a more effective point of view.

Children are very resilient and forgiving. A warm and caring teacher can make mistakes, show poor judgment, and be overly demanding without damaging a child's normal development. Inadvertent errors of judgment will occur, but kept in proper perspective they will not diminish a teacher's self-confidence or ability to make difficult classroom decisions.

Sense of Problem Solving

Successful and satisfied teachers have a strong sense of problem solving. They never discuss difficulties without proposing at least one solution. When presented with conflict or crisis, these individuals ask three questions: What are the facts? What alternatives are available? and Which alternative best fits this situation?

Only after the problem has been resolved is the question of Why examined—not to fix blame but to identify strategies to avoid future problems. Teachers with a sense of problem solving waste little time on finding fault or crying foul. They invest their energy in finding solutions to problems.

Sense of Personal Involvement

Unfortunately, a doctrine advised by many teacher educators is: Do not get personally involved in the affairs of your students. Teach them during working hours, and then go home to your own life.

A complete teacher has a strong sense of personal involvement. He or she exults when students strive and succeed and are downhearted when they fail. Such teachers are advocates and advisors and expect the best from children in their care. Students reciprocate a teacher's personal involvement and strive to meet the teacher's expectations.

Sense of Self-Worth

To work effectively with children, an individual must have a strong sense of personal value. There is no room for ambivalence about one's self-worth. Children integrate aspects of their adult mentors into their own personalities. If they are to have a strong self-concept and sense of their own value as unique human beings, their adult models must exhibit genuine feelings of worth and confidence.

COPING WITH BURNOUT

For some teachers, basic job rewards gradually dwindle and then cease. They lose their enthusiasm for leading an eager group of children through a new experience and watching as understanding replaces wonder. Satisfaction no longer results from helping frustrated fifth-graders solve a difficult arithmetic problem and then watching them independently complete a practice assignment. Teaching becomes tedious. Each day is endured, every Monday dreaded. This condition is most often referred to as *burnout.*

Burnout is a term indicating attitudinal, emotional, and physical exhaustion. It is not a sudden state but develops gradually and unnoticed until a serious problem exists. A number of general indicators point to an impending problem:

1. feelings of fatigue, depression, boredom, or apathy
2. changes in regular sleeping, eating, or exercise habits
3. irritability, forgetfulness, and inability to make decisions
4. chronic and unresolved problems with intimate relationships
5. increases in smoking, drinking, or drug use
6. increases in blood pressure, heart, and respiration rates
7. chest and back pains, headaches
8. ulcers
9. loss of interest in sex or sexual impotency
10. calling in sick, daydreaming, and not caring about the quality of one's performance
11. a general lack of concern for others; feelings of isolation
12. a noticeable lowering of self-esteem and self-confidence
13. student relationships are marked by overindulgence or harsh punishments
14. feeling controlled by the clock

Burnout is most often attributed to the effects of stress—constant, pervasive, interactive mental and emotional tension produced by environmental and personal factors. Stress is the taxing effect of the intense effort required to cope with the daily demands of living. Life is marked by change and challenge, much of which is welcome. But change always calls for some measure of readjustment and thus produces stress. Burnout then is the result of an imbalance between the demands made and one's capacity to meet them.

Environmental Stressors

Some environmental events are more stressful than others. For example, adjusting to the death of a family member, divorce, or financial failure is more difficult than dealing with job reassignment, the Christmas season, or receiving a speeding ticket. Contributing to the level of stress is the suddenness with which an event occurs, how prepared one is for it, the length of time an event lasts, the extent to which normal habits are altered, and one's perception of the event as stressful. For the teacher, job-related stressors are particularly important to recognize. The most common job-related stress factors are:

- excessive clerical work
- troublesome students
- negative attitudes of students
- time pressures
- overcrowded classes
- extracurricular duties
- inadequate salaries
- daily interruptions
- maintaining standards
- poor working conditions
- unsupportive parents

Personal Stressors

Some people seem to prefer living "on the edge," so to speak. These personalities are intense, aggressive, competitive, and ambitious. They need to race against the clock, and their life-style itself is a stressor. People of this type may be more prone to coronary disease and heart attack (and burnout) than easy-going, relaxed individuals. Such personal habits are stressors related to one's physical and mental well-being. Examples include:

- inappropriate levels of exercise (too much or too little)
- improper nutrition and diet
- disturbed or irregular sleep habits
- unhealthy use of drugs (including tobacco, alcohol, and caffeine)

Coping with Stress

One need not be a helpless victim. Stress is not immutable, and unmanaged stress is dangerous. An intense teacher who smokes, uses alcohol or other drugs regularly, and hasn't time to exercise or maintain a wholesome diet is at great risk. The combined potential for harm from personal and environmental stressors is greater than the sum of their individual potentials. Stressors interact, reinforce, and multiply each other. McBride (1983) has identified a number of general strategies for coping with stress.

1. *Develop a support system.*
   Human beings are social animals. It is important to have people who care in one's life. A close relationship with at least one other person with whom confidences can be shared is vitally important to manag-

ing stress. Isolation is an environmental stressor that interacts with personal and other factors to increase the imbalance between demand and ability to cope.

2. *Be responsible for good health.*
   Some risk factors are unavoidable, which makes preparedness the only defense. Age and heredity, for example, are given factors and beyond control. Anyone over the age of forty who has diabetes and also family members under the age of fifty who have had heart problems is inevitably more likely to develop coronary difficulties than someone who doesn't share these factors. While one cannot control such factors, he or she can influence their effect through better overall health and by reducing what may aggravate uncontrolled risks. Reducing blood pressure, smoking, cholesterol, and weight will contribute to reducing risk.

3. *Respect personal limits.*
   Teachers add unnecessary stress to their lives by taking on more than they can handle. Sometimes they agree to do a task for which they have limited skills and time. Accepting the assignment to direct the seventh-grade Christmas play with no experience or available time is guaranteed to increase stress and conflict with other faculty members. Likewise, assigning major writing assignments to all classes will tax or exceed one's energy level and commitment to read, comment, evaluate, and return every assignment within three days. The point is, know personal limits—how much time is available, what energy will be required, and what skills and talent are needed.

4. *Get an avocation.*
   Human beings can intensively focus their effort and attention on a single area for a finite period of time before quality begins to erode. Alternative activities seem to recharge the capacity to refocus. Teachers need hobbies or diversions from their teaching duties to refresh themselves.

5. *Take time off.*
   Teachers should take time off during the teaching day and after working hours, especially on weekends and during vacations. A few minutes to perform a relaxation exercise during one's preparation period or a brief game of cards during the lunch break will provide respite from the continuous routine and stress of teaching. Time away from job duties on weekends and during vacations heightens a teacher's interest in and motivation for school.

6. *Learn to "cry uncle."*

When stress pushes one to the breaking point, it becomes necessary to ask for relief. Requesting a release from a committee assignment or taking a leave of absence from an organization is often the most effective way to deal with mounting pressure. Likewise, asking for assistance in working with a particularly difficult student may reduce one's stress to a manageable level. In extreme cases, consider obtaining professional help to cope with the demands being made and the stress they are causing.

7. *Enjoy recognition of performance.*

Some people seem to feel guilty about enjoying recognition for doing a good job. Others feel shortchanged if their efforts are not appreciated or noticed. Given the two alternatives, always enjoy praise when it is given. The pleasure serves as encouragement and helps to neutralize the effects of stress.

8. *Stack the deck.*

When possible, one should take on some assignments that he or she can do well. Doing so will enhance one's reputation as a "doer" and bring recognition and praise as a competent worker. The ultimate effect is to improve one's self-concept and ability to cope with stressful events.

TIME MANAGEMENT

The one commodity equally available to everyone, without financial obligation, is time. It can't be stored, spent in advance, or retrieved once used. To speak of time management is to talk of organizing activities to fit into the time available. Certainly, many activities must be fit into a fixed timeframe—for example, work, worry, eat, and sleep. Thus, a single day is divided into work time, busy time, prime time, leisure time, and sleep time.

Timeframes

Work time is comprised of the hours each day that effort is devoted to activities associated with employment. Work effectiveness is a measure of how that time actually contributes to accomplishing the major goals of the job. A teacher who arrives at school early and stays late may be less effective in using time than the teacher who arrives later and leaves earlier but focuses more effectively on job-related activities.

Busy times are those parts of the day that are most hectic. The opening of each school day requires taking attendance, making announcements, giving instructions, and many other tasks not repeated in the balance of the day. People are less tolerant of interruption and more susceptible to stress during busy times than during normal times.

Prime time is that part of the day in which the best work is done. Some individuals do better work in the morning, some in the afternoon, and some in the evening. Teachers have the complicating factor of having students during most of the day. Whenever possible, however, planning and other high-priority tasks should be done during an individual's peak time, whenever it is.

Leisure time is reserved for nonjob-related activities, such as hobbies or entertainment. Effective use of leisure time can refresh one's mental and emotional state so that he or she continues to perform without difficulty.

Sleep time is important in warding off fatigue. Insufficient rest results in errors, inefficiency, and ineffectiveness. Regular sleep habits are critical for maintaining an even flow of energy. Short periods of rest during high levels of activity are also useful for keeping one sharp.

Principles of Time Management

Managing time more effectively requires one to eliminate some habits and replace them with new, more efficient procedures. Breaking a habit is difficult and takes considerable planning, effort, and self-discipline. There are, however, nine general time-management principles worth reviewing (Scott, 1980).

1. *Conduct a time analysis.*
   Most people want to begin managing time without doing any planning. Unfortunately, managing time has the same pitfall as developing a computer database—"garbage in garbage out." The first task of effective time management is to take inventory of how time is currently being used. This analysis can be a general description or a very detailed record. For most teachers, a general description is sufficient to begin planning. For example, jotting down a typical daily schedule might result in the following inventory for a elementary school teacher.

6:45–7:30	Arise, shower, dress, breakfast
7:30–7:50	Travel to school
7:50–8:00	Check mailbox, go to room
8:00–12:40	Teach classes
12:40–1:00	Lunch
1:00–2:30	Teach classes

2:30–3:30	Preparation and meetings
3:30–5:30	Unassigned time
5:30–6:30	Meal preparation
6:30–7:15	Evening meal
7:15–7:45	Meal clean-up
7:45–10:45	Unassigned time
10:45–11:30	Close house, prepare for sleep
11:30–6:45	Sleep

Analysis of the schedule indicates that the time between 8:00 A.M. and 3:30 P.M. is fixed. While some efficiency measures are possible, that time is committed to specific activity five days per week. The evening family meal may also be fixed to best fit family schedules. This leaves two blocks of time controlled solely by the teacher: late afternoon and late evening. At this point, one can begin to plan how to manage time. If, for example, more time is needed in the morning before school, the only alternative is to rise earlier (which may require altering the sleep schedule). The point, of course, is that altering schedules and employing time-effectiveness procedures without examining current time use will be counterproductive.

2. *Work smarter, not harder.*
   All time-management techniques are built on the notion of enabling one to get maximum results from minimum effort. Unfortunately, many individuals confuse longer hours or more practice with increased productivity. Consider Sue, who spent every available classroom moment drilling individual students. She encouraged students to come during the lunch hour and after school for additional assistance. Seth worked smarter and got better results by grouping his students and using peer tutoring to reduce the amount of time he spent in drill activities.

3. *Do central and essential jobs first.*
   Time management includes increasing the quantity of work completed and ensuring that the most important things are done. Review the day's tasks, and rank them by importance. If grades for report cards are due, that job should top the list. This technique is the keystone in a useful time-management system.

4. *Group related activities.*
   When similar jobs are grouped, daily tasks are completed much faster. Suppose one has to prepare three chapter study guides and four exercise sheets for math classes. Construct the two study guides and one exercise sheet that are needed for tomorrow, and get them out of the way at one time. Do the others as a group after completing

the priority work. In particular, group all errands (picking up duplicated materials, checking mail, delivering reports and forms) into one trip.

The school schedule doesn't provide convenient timeslots for this technique, so be creative. Work on low-priority tasks while attending committee, department, and faculty meetings. Make a series of high-priority phone calls when an adequate block of time is open, and squeeze low-priority calls into time between classes, during assemblies, or at the beginning or end of a duty period.

5. *Divide big jobs into workable steps.*
   Major tasks can appear overwhelming, which is why procrastination occurs. Take the time to divide a major task into smaller steps. If a subject-area report must be prepared and submitted for review by an accreditation committee, break it down into workable steps.

   a. Review the guidelines for preparing the report.
   b. Review the last report.
   c. List the information that must be collected.
   d. Convene the committee members and:
      1) make certain all understand the committee goals
      2) assign specific tasks to each member
      3) set timelines for completing the tasks
   e. Schedule time for typing the first draft.
   f. Read and revise the first draft; ask committee members to review and comment on the revision.
   g. Collect the comments of the committee members; prepare the final draft.

   Looking at a big job in terms of individual steps instills confidence. Proceeding step by step helps accomplish tasks on time.

6. *Use a timetable.*
   A timetable provides a spur to action. Setting a realistic deadline for completing a project makes it real. Choose or take the target completion date and work backward to develop a timetable. Go over all the activities needed to accomplish the goal, and estimate how much time each will take. Avoid unnecessary scrutiny or detail in developing the timetable. Use it as a guide, and the job will more likely be completed smoothly and on time.

7. *Concentrate on doing one thing at a time.*
   Get in the habit of concentrating effort and attention on one task at a time, even if only a few minutes are required for completion. Meeting with a colleague who is trying to prepare a test and carry on

a conversation is a waste of time; either the test or the conversation will be inadequate. Completing at least one priority task each day will add to one's energy level, help concentration, and boost feelings of personal satisfaction. Make a full finish part of the daily routine.

COPING WITH OTHER ADULTS

There is more to teaching than facilitating helping students learn. Much of the teacher's work is related to his or her ability to collaborate with other adults—administrators, colleagues, parents, and other members of students' families. Sometimes these other adults can be difficult—insensitive, obnoxious, hostile, indecisive, or vacillating. Everyone is occasionally disagreeable and thus difficult at times. A truly difficult person's behaviors, however, are consistently annoying to everyone. The most disruptive and frustrating behaviors of difficult people have been categorized by Bramson (1981).

1. Problem: Hostile-aggressives

Description.   These people attempt to bully and overwhelm others by making cutting remarks, throwing tantrums, and demanding that their wishes be met. They are abusive, abrupt, and intimidating in their personal and professional interactions. Ray, for example, was thoroughly disliked and feared by most of the high school faculty. As athletic director he had to be consulted by everyone involved in the school's athletic program. On Tuesday, Laura went to his office to deliver a transportation form, requesting permission for the cheerleading squad to ride the team bus on Friday. She handed the paper to Ray and turned to leave.

"Hold it!" Ray's voice stopped her. "Laura, you're supposed to sponsor the cheerleaders, not be one of them. How many times do I have to tell you that transportation forms are due a week before the trip?"
"Oh, geeze," he continued, "this thing is handwritten."
Laura stood silently.
"What's this?" he demanded, stabbing a finger at one word.
"Um," hesitated Laura as she craned her neck trying to see the word hidden under his finger. "I think it's—"
"Oh, go on to class," Ray dismissed her. "I'll decipher it and have Bear type a new one for you to sign."
Pale and furious, Laura hurried into the outer office.

A variation of the bully, is the sneak attacker, who does do not make a frontal approach but teases and taunts with innuendos, asides, gibes, and a host of nonverbal signals. For instance, as Sara, the guidance counselor for Glenco Elementary School, reported the school's achievement test scores to the faculty, Patricia maintained a stream of sarcasm about Sara's report, job performance, and appearance. Winking at Michelle, Patricia said, "I hope she uses better judgment counseling kids than she did selecting that dress." Michelle wished that someone would confront Pat and put a stop to her constant sniping.

Implications. Hostile-aggressives have a strong need to prove that their opinions and values are correct. They have a powerful sense of what "ought to be." The hostile-aggressive like Ron, who openly attacks, has a firm conviction that his role is to put things right. Patricia, on the other hand, is equally convinced that the supervisors or system should correct problems she points out.

Hostile-aggressive people derive their power from the reactions of their victims. The response to Ron's bullying is usually confusion, a sense of helpless frustration, anger, and physical or mental flight. The typical reaction to Patricia's behavior is resentment and a determination to avoid drawing her comments, even if it means going along with her views.

Interventions. Working with hostile-aggressives requires assertion without fighting. One cannot give in to their behavior, but at the same time an open confrontation about who is right must be avoided. Coping with Ron would require waiting for him to run down and then getting his attention (stand if sitting, sit if standing, call his name). Maintaining eye contact, state one's own opinion or position forcefully. Do not argue or try to belittle him. Rather, one should be ready to be friendly when Ron accepts him or her as an equal.

Coping with Patricia would require direct action to recognize her behavior. Avoid a confrontation by providing an alternative to conflict. Asking "That sounded like sarcasm. Was it?" gives her the opportunity to deny that an attack was intended yet serves notice that sniping will not be tolerated. If the attack is in a meeting, seek group confirmation or denial of Patricia's criticism, and then proceed to deal with any real problem she may have identified.

2. Problem: Chronic complainers

Description. Complainers find fault with everything and gripe incessantly. Even the most patient listeners find them irksome and exhausting because the hidden message is that someone (usually the listener) should do something about their problem. Skilled complainers are adept at putting others on the defensive by implying the problem is rooted in some action or inaction of theirs. While complainers often point out real problems, they do it in a manner that draws placating or defensive responses from the listener.

Implications. Complainers don't feel they are whining or annoying. They are, after all, pointing out a problem that needs solution. Unfortunately, complainers are not problem solvers because they view themselves as powerless, prescriptive, and perfect. They have come to believe that when things go well, it is because of good luck or favors from others with power. When things go wrong, they may have the solution but lack the power to effect a remedy. Thus, more powerful members of the organization must be made aware of the problem and stimulated to resolve it.

Though powerless, complainers have a clear notion of what needs to be done and a galling sense of injustice that their prescription is not being carried out. They validate themselves as good in two ways: first, by placing the responsibility for the problem resolution on another and second, by comparing their relative goodness with others' badness.

Complainers get attention but little action. Others tend to patronize, dismiss, or simply avoid them. Faced with these responses, they perceive that little or nothing is coming of their complaints and confirm their belief that they are powerless victims of unjust forces.

Interventions. Coping with a complainer can be tiring but is not difficult. Listen to the complaint attentively, even when feeling guilty or impatient. Use active listening and paraphrase perceptions of what is being said. State and acknowledge facts without comment. Do not agree or apologize, even if the allegations may actually be true. At the opportune moment move to a problem-solving mode by asking specific questions, assigning fact-finding tasks, and requesting that the complaint be made in writing.

3. Problem: Silent and unresponsive mutes

Description. Steve realized he had a problem 10 minutes after beginning the conference with Rebecca's mother. Ms. Jarvik had listened attentively to Steve's description of Rebecca's behavior problems in class and her consistent lack of effort to complete assigned work. Since then Ms. Jarvik had responded to every question or statement with a "yep," "nope," or noncommittal grunt. In desperation, Steve asked, "Ms. Jarvik, what do you suggest we do?" Ms. Jarvik wrinkled her brow and sat in silence for some time. Finally, in desperation, Steve said, "Well, here's what I suggest we do" and proceeded to outline several interventions and close the conference.

Mutes are silent, unresponsive people who won't comply when conversation or information is requested of them. Not all quiet people are mutes. Some don't converse because they are wise enough to know that nothing more needs to be added or are still processing information. The real mute, however, will not answer a direct question beyond a grunt or simple "yes" or "no."

Implications.   The mute has learned that silence has many short-term benefits. For example, unresponsiveness is a way to avoid painful interpersonal discussions and perhaps even reality. By remaining silent Ms. Jarvik did not have to acknowledge Rebecca's classroom difficulty or take responsibility for modifying it. What's more, silence is the ultimate way to wound or control people who want to communicate. They become frustrated and lose dignity. The most useful result of silence, however, is that other people make decisions or carry out interventions without further involvement from the mute. In his frustration, Steve outlined a series of interventions for which Ms. Jarvik did not have to take responsibility or even admit to the problem with Rebecca's behavior and work habits.

Interventions.   Do not attempt to interpret the meaning of the mute's silence. Only after he or she engages in dialogue can a meaningful working relationship begin. To get mutes talking ask open-ended questions and wait calmly for a response. Do not fill the silence with monologue; count the ceiling tiles if necessary. Plan enough time for the meeting to allow waiting with composure. If one must return to class or other duties within 15 or 20 minutes, the probability of accomplishing any goal is minimal. If the mute gives reaction after ample wait time, comment on what is happening, and end with another open-ended question. If the mute begins to talk, be attentive, and control the impulse to gush. If the mute refuses to engage in conversation, end the meeting, state what must and will be done about the problem, and set another appointment.

4. Problem: Congenial-amenables

Description.   Congenial-amenable people are often very personable, funny, and outgoing. They are always reasonable, sincere, and supportive in one's presence but go back on what they say or act contrary to what they have led one to expect. Dara Williams was a principal who was very much liked by her staff but also very frustrating to them. She sincerely liked all members of her faculty and conveyed her acceptance of and interest in them. She would readily listen and work to find solutions to any of their problems. Dara was caring, responsive, and agreeable until action was necessary. Then the view of the last person to talk with her would prevail. Others' influence, however unintentional, controlled her decision making.

Implications.   The congenial-amenable has terribly strong needs to be liked and accepted by others. They have learned to make others feel liked, as well, so the feelings will be reciprocated. When their needs conflict with the demands of reality, congenial-amenables are likely to agree to actions they cannot accomplish rather than risk conflict and perhaps losing a relationship. It was not unusual for Dara Williams to agree to let several grade levels conduct special activities even when the time and space obviously conflicted. The grade-level leaders then had to work out compromises and plan changes.

Interventions.   Never be insincere with or fake interest in a congenial-amenable. However, whenever possible express approval and personal interest in him or her. Make honesty nonthreatening to discourage the exchange of overstated and empty remarks. Use statements like "Ms. Williams, I really need to know where you stand on this problem because I value our great working relationship and want to avoid any misunderstandings." or "Ms. Williams, I really appreciate your positive review of my teaching performance, but even the best teachers have things that can be improved. What will you put on my written evaluation that I should improve upon?"

   Do not permit the congenial-amenable to make an unrealistic commitment. If Dara Williams approves of a class fieldtrip, and there may not be enough in the school budget, say, "There have been a lot of trips this year. I will have Ms. Jay check the budget to see if there is enough money for us to go. If there is, we will have her encumber it for us."

5. Problem: Negativists

Description.   Negativists are usually competent people but are bound to object to anyone else's creative suggestion or proposal. What differentiates the negativist from a thoughtful individual who weighs the pros and cons of a proposal is the inability to move from an objection to offering a solution. When Maryellen presented a revised music schedule to eliminate an unanticipated conflict with the third-grade lunch period, Harry immediately responded, "We tried that last year, and it just made more problems for the rest of us." Maryellen then said, "That's a good point. Is there any way to solve this without incurring last year's problems?" Harry, unable to shift to problem solving, replied, "This should have been anticipated and solved at the beginning of school."

Implications.   Negativists are convinced that any problem they do not personally attend to will not be resolved satisfactorily. They firmly believe that those in power don't care and/or are self-serving, so their negative comments are made with conviction. Further, negativists are convinced that in most cases the problems are unsolvable due to uncontrollable circumstances. Negativists can have a powerful, depressing effect on the morale and production of a group if not checked.

Interventions.   Do not try to argue a negativist out of pessimism, but make realistic statements about past successes in solving similar problems. Take time to develop and propose a solution to the problem discussed. Permit the problem to be analyzed and described in detail, allowing time for the negativist to run down before submitting the proposal. Ask, "What is the worst-case scenario that could come from this solution?" Get all the objections out for discussion.

TEACHING AS A CAREER

Public school education and educators have historically been the subjects of continuous studies, reports, and critique—especially during the 1980s. Documentation of problems and failures is voluminous, and a multitude of reforms have been proposed for improving teacher training, competence, and compensation. Subtle shifts in social values and perceptions have eroded the attractiveness of teaching as a career choice. The following reaction to Jennifer's announcement is typical.

●●●

Jennifer

Jennifer usually enjoyed coming home over school breaks, especially for Thanksgiving, when the Platts enjoyed a "family only" dinner. This holiday, however, was strained and tense. Jennifer had announced at breakfast that she intended to apply for admission to the college of education and begin the teacher-training program her junior year. Small arguments and sniping about her choice had been going on all day.

Henry Platt looked up from the turkey he was carving and declared, "Jennifer, you had a 1350 SAT and have earned a 3.8 GPA in your first two years at the university. Anybody can be a teacher, but you can be anything you want to be. You are going to waste talent that could make you a doctor or a lawyer."

Jennifer's mouth tightened, but before she could reply, her mother added, "Daddy's right, dear. With your ability you should select a career that will make a real difference to people, one where you can leave a mark of distinction."

"C'mon, Jen," said her older brother, Robert. "Think straight. You're used to a high standard of living. Dad and Mom have worked hard to build the business so we can have a good life. Nobody can make it on the money they pay teachers."

●●●

Robert is partially right. Teachers have always complained that their compensation is low relative to other careers requiring comparable training. Henry, however, is dead wrong that "Anybody can be a teacher." High test scores and a good grade-point averages don't guarantee ability to successfully teach. They are, however, promising credentials for any career choice. The fact is, good teaching requires high-quality human beings—articulate, intelligent, and caring. Teachers are able to leave a mark of distinction, as Miss Amy illustrates.

●●●

Miss Amy

The little chapel in Waverly, Iowa, had been crowded to the bursting point during the service. Now townspeople stood beneath the trees and quietly shared personal stories of Miss Amy's impact on their lives. For 32 years Miss Amy had taught more than English and literature at Waverly High School. She had modeled caring, insisted on self-discipline, and literally demanded that each of her students achieve his or her potential. Few, if any, of her students across the generations believed they were not better and more successful people for their association with her. Miss Amy had left her personal stamp on each.

●●●

The Miss Amys of education have not disappeared from classrooms, despite assertions to the contrary. Every teacher leaves a personal and positive mark on some student while others, like Miss Amy, have a gift for touching them all. It often takes teacher and student years to recognize the profound impact of a routine event, advice, or gesture. Writers or artists leave behind tangible marks of their work for others to enjoy. A talented teacher leaves an intangible mark on the heart and sensibilities of individuals to be displayed in daily values and behaviors.

Jennifer's mother didn't recognize the potential for leaving a legacy that Jennifer had accepted by choosing to be a teacher. Sherry Kroe is representative of the thousands and thousands of teachers making a real and immediate difference every day in the lives of others.

●●

Sherry

Sherry Kroe's room was finished. The bookshelves were covered with paper, the inventory completed, and all the other details required to end the school year attended. Her glance stopped on Maria's cumulative folder. "My," she thought, "what a challenge that child has been this year." Entering Sherry's third grade, Maria couldn't and wouldn't copy from the board, read, or sit in any one spot for more than a minute. The child had been downright mean, verbally and physically, to everyone around her. Sherry had chased the child, sat with her, conferred with her mother, and in moments of despair considered referring her to special education. The work and worry had paid dividends, though. By spring Maria not only could sit and copy from the board but displayed signs of becoming self-motivated. Best of all, Sherry had discovered and nurtured Maria's delightful sense of humor. At the final parent-teacher conference, Maria's mother had broken into tears as she thanked Sherry for "performing a miracle" with her child.

●●

Teachers make a difference in the lives of more than children. Entire families are affected by the school performance of their children. Making a positive difference in people isn't easy or quick. It takes hours and hours of persistent hard work to change human behavior, with no assurance that the change will stick. Perhaps this is the essence of being a teacher. A potter works with clay, color, and fire to make a beautiful, durable object. A teacher works with the intangibles of motivation, values, and intelligence to mold a unique human being while accepting that future conditions and people will reshape that uniqueness into another form.

Teaching is not an easy profession in which to succeed. It requires an orientation toward people rather than things. It demands continuous effort to improve skills. It commands confidence, self-assurance, and a positive view. The rewards, however, are worth the effort.

REFERENCES

Bramson, R. M. (1981). *Coping with difficult people.* Garden City, NY: Anchor Press.

McBride, G. (1983). Teachers, stress, and burnout. In R. E. Schmid and L. Nagata (Eds.), *Contemporary issues in special education.* New York: McGraw-Hill.

Scott, D. (1980). *How to put more time in your life.* New York: Rawson, Wade Publishers.

REFLECTIONS

1. The organization of Part III demonstrates that a host of factors determines the outcome of daily instruction. Recognizing that every teaching situation reflects some common challenges, what five initial steps might you take to assess aspects of classroom operation in need of correction?

2. Teachers can enhance student achievement by introducing recently developed strategies into classroom practices. Describe five of the strategies discussed that address low-achieving students, in particular.

3. The importance of establishing and adhering to a classroom routine and schedule that maximize opportunities for quality instruction has been well documented. Develop a schedule and list of classroom routines that would be appropriate for students at each level: elementary, middle, and high school.

4. Experience amply demonstrates that students acquire an expectation of success or failure in the classroom. Describe how you might use three motivational strategies to remedy the negative perception some students hold.

5. Sometimes disruption of the normal classroom routine is unavoidable. Describe five steps you can take to prepare students for such an occurrence.

6. As students pass through the grades, it is not unusual for them to become increasingly more responsive to classmates than to adults. Recognizing this fact, in what ways might you take advantage of the influence that students exert on one another's behavior?

7. The physical arrangement of the classroom has a significant influence on daily instruction. Draw a floorplan that reflects the current layout of your classroom. What changes might improve teaching and learning? Modify your plan to reflect appropriate changes.

8. Observe elementary, middle, and high school classrooms, and develop a comprehensive list of ways in which preventive planning tactics, expectations, discipline plans, time management, and instructional materials and methods hinder and enhance the educational program. Compare and contrast procedures across levels of schooling.

9. Develop a list of instructional procedures and groupings appropriate for students at various stages of learning. Prepare a similar list from observations in elementary, middle, and high school classrooms. Compare and contrast information on these lists.

10. In addition to the information presented in Part III, consult other appropriate textbooks and journals that address classroom instructional variables. Compare information found in these chapters with that found in the following sources:

Bliel, G. (1975). Evaluating educational materials. *Journal of Learning Disabilities*, 8, 12–19.

Bos, C. S., & Vaughn, S. (1988). *Strategies for teaching students with learning and behavior problems*. Boston: Allyn and Bacon.

Burnette, J. (1987). *Adapting instructional materials for mainstream students* (ERIC Special Project Publication/SEP).

Charles, C. M. (1983). *Elementary classroom management*. New York: Longman.

Choate, J. S., Bennett, T. Z., Enright, B. E., Miller, L. J., Poteet, J. A., & Rakes, T. A. (1987). *Assessing and programming basic curriculum skills*. Boston: Allyn and Bacon.

Collins, C. (1987). *Time management for teachers: Techniques and skills that give you more time to teach*. West Nyack, NY: Parker.

Deshler, D. A., & Graham, S. (1980). Tape recording educational materials for secondary handicapped students, *Teaching Exceptional Children*, 42, 109–110.

Evans, W. H., Evans, S. S., & Schmid, R. E. (1989). *Behavior and instructional management: An ecological approach*. Boston: Allyn and Bacon.

Evertson, C. M., Emmer, E. T., Clements, B. S., Sanford, J. P., & Worsham, M. E. (1984). *Classroom management for elementary teachers*. Englewood Cliffs, NJ: Prentice-Hall.

Gable, R. A., Hendrickson, J. M., & Lyons, S. (1987). Materials adaptation for teaching mentally retarded students. In S. Breuning & R. A. Gable (Eds.), *Advances in mental retardation and developmental disabilities* (Vol. III). Greenwich, CT: JAI Press.

Gable, R. A., Hendrickson, J. M., & Mercer, C. D. (1985). A classroom-based curriculum validation process for teaching the behaviorally disordered. In M. K. Zabel (Ed.), *Teaching: Behavior disordered youth*. Reston, VA: Council for Children with Behavior Disorders.

Gable, R. A., Hendrickson, J. M., & Young, C. C. (1987). A model for making instructional decisions for behavior disordered adolescents. In R. Rutherford, S. Forness, & C. M. Nelson (Eds.), *Severe behavior disorders of children and youth.* San Diego, CA: College-Hill.

Gall, M. (1981). *Handbook for evaluating and selecting curriculum materials*. Boston: Allyn and Bacon.

Good, R. L., & Brophy, J. E. (1987). *Looking in classrooms* (4th ed.). New York: Harper and Row.

Kerr, M. M., & Nelson, C. M. (1989). *Strategies for managing behavior problems in the classroom* (2nd ed.). Columbus, OH: Charles E. Merrill.

Lovitt, T. C., Rudsit, J., Jenkins, J. I., Pious, C., & Beneditti, D. (1986). Adapting science materials for regular and learning disabled seventh grades. *Remedial and Special Education*, 7 (1), 31–39.

Mercer, C. D., & Mercer, A. R. (1989). *Teaching students with learning problems* (3rd ed.). Columbus, OH: Charles E. Merrill.

Meyen, E., Vergason, G., & Whelan, R. (Eds.) (1983). *Promising practices for exceptional children: Curriculum implications.* Denver: Love.

Paine, S. C., Radicchi, J., Rosellini, L. C., Deutschman, L., & Darsch, C. B. (1983). *Structuring your classroom for academic success.* Champaign, IL: Research Press.

Parkay, F. W., & Hardcastle, B. (1990). *Becoming a teacher: Accepting the challenge of a profession.* Boston: Allyn and Bacon.

Reitz, A., Gable, R. A., & Trout, B. A. (1984). Education for self-control: Classroom applications of group process procedures. In R. B. Rutherford, Jr., & C. M. Nelson (Eds.), *Monograph in Behavioral Disorders* (Vol. VII). Reston, VA: Council for Exceptional Children.

Sandler, A., Arnold, L., Gable, R., & Strain, P. (1987). Effects of peer pressure on disruptive behavior of behaviorally disordered classmates. *Behavioral Disorders*, 12, 104–110.

Schulz, J. B., Carpenter, C. D., & Turnbull, A. P. (1990). *Mainstreaming handicapped students: A guide for classroom teachers* (3rd ed.). Boston: Allyn and Bacon.

Sparzo, F. J., & Poteet, J. A. (1989). *Classroom behavior: Detecting and correcting special problems.* Boston: Allyn and Bacon.

Stowitschek, J. J., Gable, R. A., & Hendrickson, J. M. (1980). *Instructional materials for exceptional children: Selection, management and adaptation.* Germantown, MD: Aspen Systems.

U.S. Department of Education. (1987). *What works: Research about teaching and learning.* (2nd ed.). Washington, DC: Author.

Wilson, J. (1990). Selecting education materials and resources. In D. Hammill & N. Bartel, *Teaching students with learning and behavior problems.* (5th ed.). Boston: Allyn and Bacon.

Index

ABOUT THE AUTHORS

WILLIAM H. EVANS is Associate Professor of Special Education at The University of West Florida. He holds a Ph.D. in special education from the University of Florida. He is a widely sought speaker, and has authored numerous articles and books such as *Assessment for Instruction* and *Behavior and Instructional Management: An Ecological Approach.* Dr. Evans has taught and continues to teach elementary, middle, and high school students.

SUSAN S. EVANS holds a Ph.D. from the University of Florida and is currently Assistant Professor of Special Education at The University of West Florida. She has served as an elementary classroom teacher, special education teacher at the elementary and middle school levels, and director of a federally funded paraprofessional training program. In addition to teaching courses in learning disabilities and assessment, Dr. Evans serves as a consulting editor for a variety of professional journals. She is a prolific writer and has authored numerous articles and books.

ROBERT A. GABLE, who holds a Ph.D. from George Peabody College, has numerous years of experience as a classroom teacher and is currently Associate Professor of Special Education at Old Dominion University. He is a well respected and prolific writer and researcher in such areas as assessment, behavioral disorders, instructional materials, and consultation and collaboration.

REX E. SCHMID is currently Supervisor of Testing for the Alachua County Schools, Gainesville, Florida. Dr. Schmid, who holds an Ed.D. from the University of Virginia, is a former special education teacher and has served as a professor of special education at Northern Iowa University and the University of Florida. As with the other authors, Dr. Schmid has authored a large number and wide variety of articles as well as books in the areas of behavioral disorders and behavior and instructional management.

READER'S REACTION

Dear Reader:

No one knows better than you the special needs of your students or the exact nature of your classroom problems. Your analysis of the extent to which this book meets *your* special needs will help us to revise this book and assist us to develop other books in the *Detecting and Correcting* series.

Please take a few minutes to respond to the questionnaire on the next page. If you would like to receive a reply to your comments or additional information about the series, indicate this preference in your answer to the last question. Mail the completed form to:

> Joyce S. Choate, Consulting Editor
> *Detecting and Correcting* Series
> c/o Allyn and Bacon
> 160 Gould Street
> Needham Heights, Massachusetts 02194

Thank you for sharing your special needs and professional concerns.

Sincerely,

Joyce S. Choate

Joyce S. Choate

READER'S REACTIONS TO
INSTRUCTIONAL MANAGEMENT
FOR DETECTING AND CORRECTING SPECIAL PROBLEMS

Name: _____   Position: _____

Address: _____   _____

_____   Date: _____

1. How have you used this book?

   ___College Text   ___Inservice Training   ___Teaching Resource

   Describe:_____

2. For which purpose(s) do you recommend its use?

3. What do you view as the major strengths of the book?

4. What are its major weaknesses?

5. How could the book be improved?

6. What additional topics should be included in this book?

7. In addition to the topics currently included in the *Detecting and Correcting* series—basic mathematics, classroom behavior, instructional management, language arts, reading, science and health, social studies, and speech and language—what other topics would you recommend?

8. Would you like to receive:

   _____a reply to your comments?

   _____additional information about this series?

Additional Comments:

THANK YOU FOR SHARING YOUR SPECIAL NEEDS AND PROFESSIONAL CONCERNS
Please send to: Joyce S. Choate, *Detecting and Correcting Series*
c/o Allyn and Bacon, 160 Gould Street, Needham Heights, Massachusetts 02194-2310